Cambridge English

Objective
Advanced

Teacher's Book
with Teacher's Resources
Audio CD/CD-ROM

Felicity O'Dell **Annie Broadhead** **Third Edition**

CAMBRIDGE UNIVERSITY PRESS
Cambridge, New York, Melbourne, Madrid, Cape Town,
Singapore, São Paulo, Delhi, Mexico City

Cambridge University Press
The Edinburgh Building, Cambridge CB2 8RU, UK

www.cambridge.org
Information on this title: www.cambridge.org/9780521181730

First published 2002
Second edition published 2008
Reprinted 2013

Printed in Poland by Opolgraf

A catalogue record for this publication is available from the British Library

ISBN 978-0-521-18173-0 Teacher's Book with Teacher's Resources Audio CD/CD-ROM
ISBN 978-0-521-18171-6 Student's Book with CD-ROM
ISBN 978-0-521-18172-3 Student's Book with answers and CD-ROM
ISBN 978-0-521-18177-8 Workbook with Audio CD
ISBN 978-0-521-18178-5 Workbook with answers and Audio CD
ISBN 978-0-521-18175-4 Class Audio CDs (2)
ISBN 978-0-521-18182-2 Student's Book Pack (Student's Book with answers and CD-ROM and Class Audio CDs (2))

Produced by Kamae Design, Oxford

Contents

Map of book 4

Exam information 7

Unit 1
Getting to know you 10

Unit 2
Keeping in touch 15

Unit 3
In the public eye 21

Unit 4
Acting on advice 26

Unit 5
Dear Sir or Madam 30

Units 1–5 Revision 34

Unit 6
Connections 35

Unit 7
A successful business 40

Unit 8
Being inventive 45

Unit 9
I have a dream 50

Unit 10
You live and learn 54

Units 6–10 Revision 57

Unit 11
Fashion statements 58

Unit 12
Leaf through a leaflet 63

Unit 13
Fact or fantasy 67

Unit 14
Evolving language 71

Unit 15
In my view ... 75

Units 11–15 Revision 78

Unit 16
What if ... ? 79

Unit 17
Rave reviews 83

Unit 18
May I introduce ...? 88

Unit 19
Do it for my sake 93

Unit 20
Feeding the mind 97

Units 16–20 Revision 100

Unit 21
Natural wonders 101

Unit 22
Under the weather 107

Unit 23
I really must insist 112

Unit 24
News and views 115

Unit 25
Intelligence 119

Units 21–25 Revision 122

Map of Objective Advanced Student's Book

TOPIC	LESSON FOCUS	EXAM SKILLS	GRAMMAR	VOCABULARY
Unit 1 **Getting to know you** 10–13 People and places	Introductions	Speaking and Listening	Conditionals	Collocations
Exam folder 1 14–15		Paper 3 Use of English: 1 Multiple-choice gap fill		
Unit 2 **Keeping in touch** 16–19 Making contact	Informal writing	Writing and Speaking	Prepositions and phrasal verbs	Multiple meanings
Writing folder 1 20–21		Informal and formal writing		
Unit 3 **In the public eye** 22–25 In the media	Interviews	Speaking	Wishes and regrets	Idioms (verb + *the* + object)
Exam folder 2 26–27		Paper 3 Use of English: 2 Open gap fill		
Unit 4 **Acting on advice** 28–31 Memory techniques	Advice and instructions	Use of English	Modals and semi- modals (1)	Prefixes and suffixes
Writing folder 2 32–33		Formal writing		
Unit 5 **Dear Sir or Madam** 34–37 Dream jobs	Formal writing	Writing and Listening	Relative clauses	Connotation
Units 1–5 Revision 38–39				
Unit 6 **Connections** 40–43 Communications technology	Phone messages	Speaking	Phrasal verbs (1)	Collocations (*have*, *do*, *make* and *take*)
Exam folder 3 44–45		Paper 3 Use of English: 3 Word formation		
Unit 7 **A successful** **business** 46–49 The world of work	Reports	Writing	Reason, result and purpose	Multiple meanings and word formation
Writing folder 3 50–51		Reports		
Unit 8 **Being inventive** 52–55 Inventions	Describing objects	Reading, Listening and Speaking	Modals and semi- modals (2)	Positive and negative adjectives
Exam folder 4 56–57		Paper 3 Use of English: 4 Gapped sentences		

TOPIC	LESSON FOCUS	EXAM SKILLS	GRAMMAR	VOCABULARY
Unit 9 **I have a dream** 58–61 Social change	Speeches	Listening	Future forms	Metaphors and idioms
Writing folder 4 62–63		Describing a novel		
Unit 10 **You live and learn** 64–67 Further study	Academic texts	Writing and Speaking	Participle clauses	Word formation
Units 6–10 Revision 68–69				
Unit 11 **Fashion statements** 70–73 Fashion	Articles	Listening and Speaking	Reported speech	Collocation
Exam folder 5 74–75		Paper 3 Use of English: 5 Key word transformations		
Unit 12 **Leaf through a leaflet** 76–79 Making decisions	Information pages	Listening	-*ing* forms	Verbs with the -*ing* form
Writing folder 5 80–81		Information sheets		
Unit 13 **Fact or fantasy** 82–85 Dreaming	Short stories	Writing	Past tenses and the present perfect	Adjectives and adjectival order
Exam folder 6 86–87		Paper 1 Reading: 1 Themed texts		
Unit 14 **Evolving language** 88–91 Human communication	Lectures	Listening and Use of English	The passive; *to have/ get something done*	Word formation
Writing folder 6 92–93		Essays		
Unit 15 **In my view ...** 94–97 Family life	Expressing opinions	Speaking	The infinitive	Agreeing and disagreeing
Units 11–15 Revision 98–99				
Unit 16 **What if ... ?** 100–103 Mini sagas	Competition entries	Writing	Hypothesising	Idioms of the body
Exam folder 7 104–105		Paper 1 Reading: 2 Gapped text		
Unit 17 **Rave reviews** 106–109 The arts	Reviews	Speaking	Articles	Giving opinions
Writing folder 7 110–111		Reviews		

TOPIC	LESSON FOCUS	EXAM SKILLS	GRAMMAR	VOCABULARY
Unit 18 **May I introduce ...?** 112-115 White lies	Small talk	Writing and Speaking	Emphasising	Collocations and longer chunks of language
Exam folder 8 116–117		Paper 1 Reading: 1, 3 and 4 Multiple choice and multiple matching		
Unit 19 **Do it for my sake** 118–121 Persuasion	Proposals	Writing and Speaking	Language of persuasion	Multiple meanings
Writing folder 8 122–123		Proposals		
Unit 20 **Feeding the mind** 124–127 Food, pictures and science	Talks	Listening and Writing	Inversion	Word formation
Units 16–20 Revision 128–129				
Unit 21 **Natural wonders** 130–133 Beauty spots	Travel articles	Writing and Speaking	Range of grammatical structures	Idioms
Exam folder 9 134–135		Paper 4 Listening		
Unit 22 **Under the weather** 136–139 Climate change	Interpreting facts and figures	Reading and Speaking	Interpreting and comparing	Weather and Climate
Writing folder 9 140–141		Persuasive writing		
Unit 23 **I really must insist** 142–145 Putting your point across	Formal letters	Listening, Writing and Speaking	Phrasal verbs (2)	Language for complaining
Exam folder 10 146–147		Paper 5 Speaking		
Unit 24 **News and views** 148–151 Stories in the news	Investigative journalism	Listening	Connecting words	Choosing language
Writing folder 10 152–153		Articles		
Unit 25 **Intelligence** 154–157 Intelligence and studies	Texts dealing with theory	Writing and Speaking	Complex sentences and adverbial clauses	Research and experiments
Units 21–25 Revision 158–159				
Grammar Folder 163–176				

Content of Cambridge English: Advanced

Cambridge English: Advanced, also known as Certificate in Advanced English (CAE) consists of five papers, each of which is worth 20% of the exam total. It is not necessary to pass all five papers in order to pass the examination. There are three passing grades: A, B, C. As well as being told your grade, you will also be given a statement of your results which shows a graphical profile of your performance on each paper.

Extended certification

Cambridge English: Advanced is set at Level C1 of the Common European Framework of Reference for Languages (CEFR). Extended certification can give you additional credit for the language skills you demonstrate in the exam. It works in two ways.
- If you perform particularly well, you can get credit at a higher level on the CEFR. If you get grade A in the exam, you receive a certificate indicating that you are at C2 level.
- You can also receive credit for your English language skills, even if you do not achieve a passing grade. So if you do not get enough marks for a grade C in the exam, you can still be awarded a certificate showing performance at level B2 if you show this level of ability in the exam.

Results	CEFR level
Grade A	C2
Grades B and C	C1
B2 level	B2

Paper 1 Reading 1 hour 15 minutes

There are four parts to this paper and they are always in the same order. Each part contains one or more texts and a comprehension task. The texts used are from newspapers, magazines, journals, books, leaflets, brochures, etc.

Part	Task Type	Number of Questions	Task Format	Objective Exam folder
1	Multiple choice	6	You read three short texts relating to the same theme and have to answer two multiple-choice questions on each. Each question has four options, A, B, C and D.	6 (86–87)
2	Gapped text	6	You must read a text with extracts removed. You need to use the missing extracts to complete the text.	7 (104–105)
3	Multiple choice	7	You read a text followed by multiple-choice questions with four options.	8 (116–117)
4	Multiple matching	15	You read a text, which may be divided into sections, or a group of short texts, preceded by multiple-matching questions. You match a question to the part of the text where you can find the information.	8 (116–117)

Paper 2 Writing 1 hour 30 minutes

There are two parts to this paper. Part 1 is compulsory as you have to answer it in 180–220 words. In Part 2 there are five questions, two of which relate to set texts. You must write an answer of 220–260 words to one of these five questions.

Part	Task Type	Number of Tasks	Task Format	Objective Writing Folder
1	article report proposal letter	1	You are given a situation and some information which you need to respond to. You may be given two different pieces of material which you need to use in your answer.	1 Informal writing (20–21) 2 Formal writing (32–33) 3 Reports (50–51) 8 Proposals (122–123) 10 Articles (152–153)
2	article report review essay letter proposal information sheet competition entry contribution to a longer piece (only the first four from this list used for set text tasks)	Choose 1 from a choice of four tasks.	You are given a choice of tasks which specify the type of text you have to write, your purpose for writing and the person or people you have to write for.	4 Set texts (62–63) 5 Information sheets (80–81) 6 Essays (92–93) 7 Reviews (110–111) 9 Persuasive writing (140–141)

Paper 3 Use of English 1 hour

There are five parts to this paper, which tests your grammar and vocabulary.

Part	Task Type	Number of Questions	Task Format	Objective Exam Folder
1	Multiple-choice gap fill mainly testing vocabulary	12	Multiple-choice gap fill mainly testing vocabulary. Each question has four options: A, B, C and D.	1 (14–15)
2	Open gap fill, mainly testing grammar	15	You fill each of 15 gaps in a text with one word each.	2 (26–27)
3	Word formation	10	You need to use the right form of a given word to fill the gaps in a text containing 10 gaps.	3 (44–45)
4	Gapped text	5	You read three sentences. Each sentence has a gap. You must write one word which is appropriate in all three sentences.	4 (56–57)
5	Key word transformations	8	You read a given sentence, and then complete a second sentence so that it has a similar meaning to the first one. You can use between three and six words, including one word which is given.	5 (74–75)

Paper 4 Listening approximately 40 minutes

There are four parts to this paper. All the recordings are heard twice. The recordings are set in a variety of situations. In some parts you hear just one speaker; in others more than one speaker.

Part	Task Type	Number of Questions	Task Format	Objective Exam Folder
1	Multiple choice	6	You hear three short extracts and have to answer two multiple-choice questions on each. Each question has three options, A, B and C.	**9** (134–135)
2	Sentence completion	8	You hear a recording and have to write a word or short phrase to complete sentences.	**9** (134–135)
3	Multiple choice	6	You hear a recording and have to answer multiple-choice questions with four options.	**9** (134–135)
4	Multiple matching	10	You hear five short extracts. There are two matching tasks focusing on the gist and the main points of what is said, the attitude of the speakers and the context in which they are speaking.	**9** (134–135)

Paper 5 Speaking 15 minutes

There are four parts to this paper. There are usually two of you taking the examination together and two examiners. This paper tests your grammar and vocabulary, interactive communication, pronunciation and how you link your ideas.

Part	Task Type	Time	Format	Objective Exam Folder
1	Three-way conversation between two students and one of the examiners	3 minutes	The examiner asks you both some questions about yourself and your interests and experiences.	**10** (146–147)
2	Individual 'long turn' with brief response from partner	4 minutes	You are each given some visual and written prompts and the examiner will ask you to talk about these for about a minute. You are asked to give a short response after your partner has finished their 'long turn'.	**10** (146–147)
3	Collaborative task	4 minutes	You are given some visual prompts for a discussion or decision-making task and you discuss these prompts with your partner.	**10** (146–147)
4	Three-way interaction between students and one of the examiners	4 minutes	The examiner asks you and your partner questions relating to topics arising from Part 3.	**10** (146–147)

1 Getting to know you

GENRE: Introductions
TOPIC: People and places

Speaking	People and culture
Grammar	Conditionals
Reading	Culture shock
Vocabulary	Collocations
Listening	Meeting people

Workbook contents

Reading	Putting paragraphs into gaps
Vocabulary	Collocations
Grammar	Conditionals
Writing	A personal description

Student's Book pages 10–13

Lesson planning

Throughout the Teacher's Book, guidance is given relating to the length of lesson: SV (short version) and LV (long version). The SV gives an indication of what can be cut out of the lesson if time is short or which parts could be set for homework. The LV gives suggestions on what could be developed and provides extension activities where appropriate.

SV   Conditionals exercise 3 could be set for homework.
LV   See extension activities in the Speaking section.

Speaking

Introduce Unit 1 by asking students questions such as:

- *Which English-speaking country do you know the most about?*
- *Are you curious about other countries and cultures?*
- *To what extent is learning about countries and their cultures part of learning a language?*

Generate a class discussion using these questions and establish that in order to appreciate a language fully, some knowledge of the culture of the country where it is spoken can be an advantage. However, do not spend too much time on the discussion at this point as it is important to move on to the questions in the Student's Book and establish a lively pace.

1   The aim of exercises 1 and 2 is to generate interest in places. It allows students to bring their own knowledge to the class. If this is your first lesson with the class, you can do exercise 1 as a whole-class activity. Alternatively, you could ask students to do exercise 1 in small groups.

As you go through the answers, elicit students' knowledge of the places shown.

Answers
A Sydney, Australia
B Tokyo, Japan
C Berlin, Germany

2   Ask the students to read the blog extracts quickly and match them to the cities in the photos. Explain that it is not necessary to understand every word.

Answers
1 A
2 C
3 B

Extension activity

The ideas in exercises 1 and 2 could be developed further by asking the students to prepare questions about countries they know. This could be part of a long-term project in which students research another country.

3   Give students about five minutes to think about a place and to make notes. Encourage them not to write full sentences at this stage, only to write ideas and useful words.

4   Put students in pairs. Encourage them to ask each other questions to find out more information. Get feedback from the whole class, asking students to say something interesting about what their partner said.

Extension activity

Students write a short text describing a town they know well, either in groups in class or for homework.

Teaching extra

Promote learner independence by eliciting information and thereby acknowledging what students already know. Guide them to find out background information or information about the language for themselves.

5 Ask students to work with a different partner and discuss the questions. When they have finished question d, elicit phrases from the class and write them on the board.

Give feedback on question e. Many people show their interest in listening to a speaker by making eye contact, leaning a little towards the speaker and using facial expressions such as nodding or shaking their head. Then there may be lots of *aha*, *mm* and *yeah* noises. Asking students to act out their suggestions for question b can be fun.

Extension activity

The Exam spot draws attention to the fact that social English is helpful both in real life and in Part 1 of the Speaking test (Paper 5). Go through the Exam spot with the students and then ask them to prepare some questions to find out more about their partner. Point out that the questions can be phrased openly, e.g. *Tell me something about your family*. If necessary, give some examples such as: *What do you like to do in your free time? What sort of job do you hope to do in the future?*

Conditionals

The Grammar folder at the back of the Student's Book provides explanations and further examples. The grammar here is covered on page 163.

1 Read out the example of the zero conditional and then refer to the table of conditional forms. Ask students to complete the rest of the table.

Answers

Type	Tense – *if* clause	Tense – main clause	Use to talk about ...
zero	present simple / continuous	present simple / continuous	common states or events
first	present simple / continuous	*will / to be / going to /* present simple or continuous	possible states or events
second	past simple / continuous	*would* + infinitive without *to*	hypothetical or very unlikely situations
third	past perfect	*would have* + past participle	the past, and say that it is impossible to do anything about it now

2 This exercise introduces some of the more advanced forms of conditionals.

Possible answers
a If you have any difficulties, I'll be available to help.
b If it hadn't been for Jane's intervention, / If Jane hadn't intervened, the meeting would have gone on far too long.
c I'll open the window if it'll make you feel more comfortable.

3 Ask students to work on their own and then check their answers with a partner.

Answers
a If so   b otherwise   c Given   d unless
e Provided

Corpus spot

Corpus spots throughout the book highlight some of the typical errors that students at this level make in the exam.

Go through the Corpus spot with students. As in other Corpus spots in this book, this language area has been identified in the Cambridge English Corpus as an area in which learners often need extra practice. The Corpus is a collection of over 100,000 exam scripts from Cambridge ESOL providing over 45 million words of data, and it shows the real mistakes candidates have made in their exams. The mistakes the authors focus on are typical of learners at C1/C2 level and that is why the course provides further practice in using these features of the language accurately.

Reading

1 This exercise encourages cross-cultural awareness. Ask students to discuss the questions with a partner. Ask them to make notes of the main points of their discussion so that they can report back to the rest of the class when they have finished.

2 Ask students to read the blog and then answer the questions.

> **Answers**
> a Some cultural differences are easy to see; they are 'on the surface'. This is the tip of the iceberg. However, below the surface there are many deeper differences, beliefs and attitudes, which are more difficult to understand. This is the larger part of the 'iceberg' which is under the surface.
> b Find out as much as you can before going, and then try to make contact with real people.

3 Ask students to discuss the questions in small groups.

> **Possible answers**
> a It can be dangerous to make sweeping statements about a nationality, as every nation is made up of a wide range of individuals. General statements will probably be untrue for at least some of the people. If the characteristics are negative, it may be offensive to voice them.
> b students' own answers

Vocabulary

Go through the Vocabulary spot, which explains what collocation is.

1 Refer back to the blog and point out where the collocations are.

> **Answers**
> a *culture shock* = noun–noun
> b *make a decision* = verb–noun
> c *incredibly exciting* = adverb–adjective
> d *acceptable behaviour* = adjective–noun

2 Ask students to work in pairs and find some more examples.

> **Suggested answers**
> face the challenge; way of life; set off on (my) adventure; totally new; weekend getaway; sense of humour; really interesting; read between the lines; cultural references; look up information; make friends

3 Ask students to work with a partner or in small groups. If this is the first time your students have done this sort of exercise, go through the example carefully. If students need further help, give them the first letter of each missing word.

> **Suggested answers**
> face; relish; take up **a challenge**
> **set off on** an adventure; a trip; a journey/voyage
> brand; almost/nearly; completely/totally **new**
> make; see; keep/stay in touch with **a friend**
> fairly; incredibly/really/particularly/extremely; not remotely **interesting**

Listening

Go through the information in the Exam spot. This task is slightly different from the actual exam; here there are only seven options. (The actual exam has eight options to choose from.) This should make the task slightly easier for students.

1 Ask students to look at the photos of places and as a class, speculate about where these places might be and what it would be like to live there.

1 01 Go through the instructions. Play the recording and ask students to match the speakers to the photos.

> **Answers**
> 1 D   2 E   3 B   4 A   5 C

> **Recording script**
> **Speaker 1:** We went to this incredible place, a place which has one of the largest mosques in the whole of North Africa. We went in and then some boys came and, er, they wanted to show us around. Well, we weren't so sure, but they did anyway. After that, they asked us to come to a carpet museum, and they said, really, you have to see – it's wonderful, there are old Tunisian carpets. So we decided to go with them. And guess what! The museum turned out to be a carpet shop, owned by the father of one of the boys. And of course, he wanted to sell us a carpet. We actually didn't want to buy one because we didn't have enough space in our backpacks, but finally he managed to persuade us to buy one. So my friend, yeah, she bought one. To thank us for that, the boys guided us around the town and we ended up going down these really narrow alleyways, and we had no idea where we were because this whole city was like a maze. Then we came to a house and we realised it was the house of one of the boys and we were invited in by his family and we had tea, coffee, nice biscuits, and it was a really, really good experience.

Speaker 2: My story is actually a bit bizarre. I was going to Florida and during the flight I had to go to the bathroom. And in front of me there was a woman, she was about, maybe 50, who went into the bathroom, but she didn't lock the door, it was still on the er, ... it wasn't completely locked. And I thought that maybe I should knock on the door and tell her that her door wasn't completely closed, but I didn't. And I also had a funny feeling that this wouldn't turn out well. And I was right because a little later the door flew open and there she was, and she gave out a loud shriek and me and the rest of the line just stood there in disbelief, totally in shock.

Speaker 3: Four years ago I was in Indonesia. First, I went to Sumatra and er, there I met a man who wanted to show us his village. So we went off with him. The village was very small, perhaps 500 inhabitants, maybe less. And they had these houses, wooden houses, with the roof shaped like a boat. And it was very special because the people there had never seen tourists before. So they acted like, erm, they treated us like very special people, which we aren't, of course. They were a bit shy at first but then somehow we managed to communicate, and what I realised is that people, good people, are the same perhaps the world over.

Speaker 4: Well, it was supposed to be a weekend trip with the rowing club. It was in the middle of winter. When we got there we couldn't even get out on the water, it was way too cold and we were in this big, er, shed, the size of a football pitch. There was no heating, the water was coming through the roof. The whole time it was windy and terrible. We went there by bike and it took us about three hours to get there, I think. And we just, you know, went on automatic pilot and went on and on and on. And in this shed we couldn't get warm and people started getting really irritable and we started fighting over stupid, stupid things, for example, who has to cook dinner, who has to do the dishes, and we were really nasty to each other. And we had to sleep all together in one corner otherwise we'd freeze to death. There were about 25 of us all huddled together, trying to sleep and hating each other.

Speaker 5: Whenever people talk about dolphins, they always say they're very intelligent creatures but I never really grasped the idea of how intelligent they are until recently. There's this place in Zanzibar, off Africa, where it's possible to go swimming with dolphins. When you go down to the bay, you can meet up with these people that you go on a boat with, and even before you've seen anything, their enjoyment really rubs off on you. They're laughing all the time and when they find some dolphins,

they're really proud of themselves because they've found some dolphins and they know that you're really going to love it. What you have to do then is, you have to jump in the water, when the boat stops you jump in the water, and if you're lucky, the dolphins come straight at you, and then they dive really deep in the water so you can't see them any more. They hide themselves and then they come back. And when you see the look in their eyes, you see they're just making fun of you! And for me, that's proof of how smart dolphins really are.

2 **1 01** Ask students to read through the topic headings. Play the recording again and ask students to match the speakers to the topics. In the exam, students have to do both tasks as they listen to the recording twice.

Answers

1 E	2 C	3 F	4 A	5 G

3 Ask students to discuss this question in small groups or as a class. If you have extra time, you could encourage students to talk about some of their own adventures.

Exam folder 1

Student's Book pages 14–15

Paper 3 Part 1
Multiple-choice gap fill

Remind students that there is a full description of the exam on pages 7–9 of the Student's Book. Paper 3 has five parts and candidates have one hour to complete the paper. The Exam folders can be studied by students on their own outside class, but notes are given below for a mini-lesson in class.

Explain that the test focus in Paper 3 Part 1 is vocabulary. Point out that the general area of vocabulary can be subdivided into categories such as phrasal verbs, collocations and idioms and that the exam tests a range of different vocabulary areas.

Go through the examples of the types of words and expressions which can be tested. If you have a dictionary of collocations and a dictionary of phrasal verbs, it would be useful to show them to the students at this point. Then go through the Exam information box. This gives students strategies for tackling this part of Paper 3.

Go through the task *My aunt's kitchen*, asking students to follow all the steps in the Exam information box.

Answers
1. A (*stale* collocates with *cigarette smoke*)
2. B (*piled* = put in an ordered heap)
3. D (*built-in* = fixed to the wall)
4. B (*crockery* = cups, plates, etc.)
5. B (*pull a door* = close)
6. C (*fond* goes with the preposition *of*)
7. D (*buy in* collocates with *bulk*)
8. A (a cake can be cut into *slices* or *pieces*)
9. C (*make someone feel at* collocates with *home*)
10. D (*scattering* = letting them fall in many different directions)
11. D (*faded* = old, with a pattern which is no longer clear)
12. B (*scent* has a positive connotation and collocates with *lovely*)

2 Keeping in touch

GENRE: Informal writing
TOPIC: Making contact

Speaking	Keeping in touch
Writing	Informal writing
Grammar	Prepositions and phrasal verbs
Vocabulary	Multiple meanings
Listening	Note taking
Speaking	Developing what you want to say

Workbook contents

Writing	Informal letter/email
Listening	Discussions about language use
Vocabulary	Phrasal verbs
Grammar	Prepositions and phrasal verbs

Student's Book pages 16–19

Lesson planning

SV Prepositions and phrasal verbs, exercises 2 or 4 could be set for homework.

LV See extension activities in the Prepositions and phrasal verbs and Listening sections.

Speaking

1 Ask students to work with a partner to discuss the questions, which introduce the topic of the unit. Leave time for a class round-up of the students' discussions.

2 The aim of this question is to raise awareness about the reasons for writing informal letters or emails. Ask the students to read the email quickly and answer the question. Elicit the answer from the whole class.

Suggested answers
to give information about finishing exams
to thank a friend for a present
to give information about a holiday

Writing

1 Go through the information in the Exam spot. Explain that if you know who the intended reader is, it should be clear which style, formal or informal, is suitable for the letter. It is also important that the purpose for writing is clear to the reader. Ask students to read the email again in order to answer questions a–e.

Suggested answers
a beginnings: *Dear Sarah, Hello Sarah*; endings: *See you, Love and kisses, Lots of love, All the best*
b It resembles spoken English, e.g. *Anyway, ...*; it uses informal vocabulary, e.g. *grab* instead of *steal/take*; it uses rhetorical questions (e.g. *It's a hard life, isn't it?*) to engage the reader.
c use of dashes to indicate a pause; brackets to denote an aside; exclamation marks
d yes
e Paragraph 1: I've gone from the stress of exams to the quiet of a holiday in a remote place.
Paragraph 2: Thank you for the present.
Paragraph 3: I'm going to explore other parts of the island tomorrow.

2 Go through the message with students, then ask them to order the sample sentences in pairs.

Answers
1 Sorry for not writing back earlier.
2 I've been rehearsing for a play.
3 I'm going to be studying for a new clarinet exam.
4 Will you stay on at the hotel in the holidays?
5 How much longer do you have on your course?

Question b is very similar to the type of task candidates could find in the Writing test (Paper 2). The number of words required in the examination is approximately 200, but here the focus is more on content and style than on length. Students could work with a partner, in small groups, as a class with you writing up their sentences on the board, or the question could be set as homework, depending on how much guidance your students need.

Prepositions and phrasal verbs

The language here is covered on page 163 of the Grammar folder.

1 Go through the introduction in the Student's Book. Encourage students to find other phrasal verbs in the email and to deduce their meaning from context.

> **Suggested answers**
> *go with* = match/combine
> *look at* = look/examine
> *go up* = travel (especially north)
> *come back* = return
> *call in* = visit
> *go for* = sell for
> *go out* = leave

2 This exercise could be set for homework.

> **Answers**
> a I tried to get you **on** your mobile but it was switched off.
> b My brother's just got married **to** my best friend and they're going to live in New York.
> c I'm looking forward **to** hearing all your news.
> d I need to buy a new jacket to go **with** my blue trousers.
> e How did you get **on** in the interview you went to?
> f I think I was beginning to get stuck **in** a rut in my home town.
> g I wonder if you could come up **with** some suggestions.
> h It's an idea that might catch **on** if people read a lot about it on Twitter.
> i I'm afraid you can't always trust the trains to run **on** time.
> j Some of the students couldn't come **to** the pub because they are underage.
> k I'm not sure if I'll get the job, but I'm going to go **for** it anyway.
> l Tom's a doctor and seems to be **on** duty most weekends.

Corpus spot

Go through the Corpus spot box. Ask them to correct the sentences, paying special attention to the prepositions.

> **Answers**
> a ... get on well with people ~~from~~ of ...
> b ... get off ~~on~~ at ...
> c ... background knowledge ~~on~~ of ...
> d ... travel back ~~to~~ in time.
> e ... put a lot of effort ~~to~~ in/into ...
> f the pleasure ~~in~~ of ...

3 Answering this question reinforces the notion that all texts have been written to convey meaning or feelings; they should not be seen merely as exam practice. Make sure that students read the whole text first before they start to fill the gaps. This technique will stand them in good stead for the exam.

> **Suggested answers**
> **Pros:** we can keep in touch with people all around the world more easily; information is more readily available; companies can reach more customers.
> **Cons:** our personal information and money may be more at risk; harassment may increase.

4

> **Answers**
>
> | | | | |
> |---|---|---|---|
> | 1 | with | 9 | to/for |
> | 2 | away | 10 | in |
> | 3 | to | 11 | of |
> | 4 | across | 12 | for |
> | 5 | around/round/across | 13 | on |
> | 6 | in | 14 | with |
> | 7 | with | 15 | In |
> | 8 | with | 16 | against |

 Extension activity

Ask students to find another text, preferably from an authentic source, and ask them to rewrite a passage deleting the prepositions and adverbs. They then give their passage to another student to complete.

Teaching extra

Encourage students to read in English. They could read either graded readers or authentic texts such as novels, magazines or online articles. Students can then use these sources for extension activities such as the one above.

5 These questions round off this section by personalising the situation for students. Get feedback from the whole class once students have finished their discussion.

Vocabulary

Go through the Vocabulary spot, which explains what is meant by multiple meanings. Point out that an awareness of this feature of English vocabulary can help students to build up a richer vocabulary. Encourage them to check for multiple meanings whenever they look up words in a dictionary.

1   If your students find this exercise difficult, you could give them the first letter of the missing word and/or the number of letters in the missing word.

Answers
a	foot	d	round
b	last	e	answer
c	power	f	ran

Listening

1   The aim of this listening is to provide a model of authentic speech similar in topic to Part 1 of the Speaking test (Paper 5). Encourage speculation about the students' lives based on the photos.

2   **1 02** Ask students to work with a partner; one should listen to Yolanda's answers and the other to Martin's. Play the first part of the recording. When they have finished making notes, students exchange information. Encourage them to write key words, not full sentences. Accept any correct details. The aim is for students to see that answers are usually developed. Point out that it will not be possible to write down everything students hear, so notes will be sufficient.

Suggested answers
Yolanda
Where are you from?	Spain	50km north of Madrid
What languages have you studied in the past?	Russian	difficult – gave up

Martin
Where are you from?	Germany	now lives in France
What languages have you studied in the past?	French and Italian	Spanish when he went to Spain on holiday

3   **1 03** Play the next part of the conversation.

Suggested answers
Yolanda
hobbies	watching DVDs	Invite friend round and watch DVDs together Doesn't go to cinema – too expensive, there isn't one nearby likes thrillers/suspense because you can get lost in a good plot
future hopes	travel to Australia	recommended by a friend – good lifestyle, can do sporty things
living or working abroad permanently	not sure	likes living in Spain because of the weather in summer, relaxed lifestyle
earliest memories of school	school report	wanted to open report but didn't want to disobey teacher; parents pleased with report

Martin
hobbies	concerts and cinema has just taken up karate	not much time for hobbies karate trains the body and the mind
future hopes and dreams	finish studies get a job have a family	job in large multi-national so that he can travel
living or working abroad permanently	yes	Northern Europeans live to work; people in Mediterranean countries work to live
earliest memories of school	a maths task	wasn't doing task, others went to watch TV; then he completed the task quickly – made him a good student

Extension activity

Photocopy the recording script on page 18 and ask students to highlight the phrases which Yolanda and Martin used to develop their answers.

4   Ask students this question to round off the activity.

Recording script

Yolanda: Hi, I'm Yolanda. I'm from Spain.

Martin: Hi, nice to meet you. I'm Martin. I'm originally from Germany, but I live in France now because my dad works there.

Yolanda: Wow, that's interesting. I've lived about 50 kilometres north of Madrid all my life.

Martin: Your English is pretty good.

Yolanda: Thanks, that's what I'm studying at the moment. I studied Russian for a while but I found it very difficult and gave up.

Martin: I did French and Italian at school and then I learnt a little bit of Spanish when I went on holiday in Spain.

Yolanda: What do you do in your free time?

Martin: Mm. My hobby is going to concerts and going to the cinema. I know it's not much but I don't really have a lot of time for hobbies. Do you like going to the cinema?

Yolanda: Well, I don't go to the cinema that often, partly because it's quite expensive and partly because there isn't one close to where I live. But what I like doing is getting a DVD and then inviting friends round to watch it with me.

Martin: What sort of films do you like watching?

Yolanda: I like thrillers, suspense, that kind of thing. I like it when you get totally involved with a good plot. What else do you do in your free time?

Martin: I've just taken up karate because I think it trains both your body and your mind.

Yolanda: I think that's a good aim. What other aims have you got for the future?

Martin: Well, for the short-term future I'm going to finish my studies and then the idea is to get a job in a large multinational company where I'll have the opportunity to travel for my job. I sometimes wonder if that doesn't match my other more long-term ambition, which is to settle down and have a family. Would you like to travel?

Yolanda: Absolutely, I'd love to go to Australia because I have a friend who went on holiday there and she said the lifestyle is great. People are really into sport and the climate's perfect for lots of outdoor things. But I don't know how I'd feel about living or working abroad permanently. Could you do that?

Martin: Yeah, I can see myself ending up in a foreign country for a long time. But I think in England, Germany and all of northern Europe, people like, work all the time, and people, especially in Mediterranean countries, people work to live and we live to work and we need to get back to that same kind of philosophy that they have.

Yolanda: I don't know if I could live abroad permanently and I must admit I like living in Spain with its warm, sunny summers. And I think you're right, the people are more relaxed. Like you say, you can get stressed out if you're studying or working, but then when you've finished, you know, you've got a good few hours of sunshine left and you can go outside. I remember when I was at primary school, I loved going home to play in the garden in summer.

Martin: Wow, you've got a good memory if you can remember being at primary school. What's your earliest memory of school?

Yolanda: My earliest memory is when I was in primary school, and every term you got a report to take home. And I remember the teacher saying, whatever you do, you must not open this report, it must go home to your parents. And I remember I was dying to open it but I was scared of disobeying the teacher. Anyway, when I gave it to my parents, they were pleased because it was a good report.

Martin: Actually, I think my earliest memory is in primary school as well. I was supposed to be doing this maths task but I was being lazy and couldn't be bothered to start it. Everyone else had gone off to watch this TV programme that we were allowed to watch once a week. And the teacher said, you've got to stay here and finish this. So I thought, right then, and I did the maths problem in about 10 seconds. I remember thinking, I should have just done my work in the first place. Perhaps realising that at an early age turned me into a good student!

Speaking

The aim here is to encourage students to develop their spoken answers.

1   If possible, elicit answers from the class as a whole and write up students' suggestions on the board.

> **Suggested answer**
> A good communicator asks questions, takes turns, listens, develops answers and uses appropriate body language.

2   Ask students to read the Exam spot, then to work with a partner and suggest how answers to questions a–d could be developed.

> **Suggested answers**
> a   talk about the size of the city, its facilities/amenities
> b   pleasure, future job, studies
> c   places visited / cinema / theatre / concert – why it was interesting
> d   work, study, family, travel, ambitions

3   Ask students to work in groups of three. Go through the instructions in the Student's Book. Draw this table on the board for students to copy. Ask Students A to fill it in as Students B and C are speaking.

Main idea Student B	Main idea Student C	Extra information Student B	Extra information Student C

Make sure time is allowed for feedback either within groups or to the class as a whole. If you feel that students need more practice, ask them to swap roles and repeat the task.

4   This question is included so that students know how they are going to be assessed for the Speaking test. See the Teaching extra for further information.

Teaching extra

All details about the examination can be found at www.cambridgeesol.org/exams/cae

The assessment criteria for speaking are as follows.

Grammatical resource

Students are awarded marks for the accurate and appropriate use of a range of both simple and complex forms.

Vocabulary resource

Students are expected to use a range of appropriate vocabulary to meet the task requirements, for example, to speculate and exchange views.

Discourse management

Examiners are looking for evidence of the candidate's ability to express ideas and opinions in coherent, connected speech.

Pronunciation

Students are assessed on their ability to produce both individual sounds and prosodic features (i.e. linking of words, stress and intonation to convey intended meaning).

Interactive communication

Examiners are looking for the use of strategies to maintain interaction (e.g. conversational turn-taking).

Writing folder 1

Student's book pages 20–21

Informal and formal writing

1 This activity can be done with the whole class or in small groups.

> **Answers**
> A informal, a friend writing to a friend – giving news about holiday plans – promising to tell him/her about the holiday when he/she returns
> B formal, a college writing to a course applicant – apologising for the delay in replying and confirming the applicant's place on the course and that information will be sent out soon
> C informal, a friend writing to a friend – regretting the fact that the friend could not go to a party as he/she was ill – giving news about who was at the party and hoping the friend is feeling better
> D formal, a film club confirming receipt of a member's application form and information that a receipt will be sent once the membership fee has been paid.

2 The aim is for students to become aware of the features of informal letters.

> **Answers**
> b opening sentence, referring back to a previous letter (formal)
> c apologising for delay in replying (informal)
> d apologising for delay in replying (formal)
> e thanking for a previous last letter (neutral)
> f thanking for a party (informal)
> g thanking for a wedding invitation (neutral)
> h thanking for a book (neutral)

3

> **Suggested answers**
> **refusing an invitation**
> *Oh no! I'm sorry I can't come to your party because I'll be on holiday.* (informal)
> *I'm afraid I am unable to attend due to a prior arrangement.* (formal)
>
> **congratulating**
> *Wow, well done you – you passed your driving test first time!* (informal)
> *Congratulations on passing your examination.* (formal)
>
> **giving your opinion**
> *I think …* (informal)
> *In my opinion …* (formal)
>
> **giving advice**
> *Why don't you …* (informal)
> *I think you should …* (formal)

4 It can be very useful for students to build up a stock of set phrases to use or adapt in the Writing test.

> **Answers**
> a would, grateful, could, further
> b acknowledge, receipt
> c enclose, self-addressed
> d would, appreciate, response
> e forward, hearing, earliest convenience

> ### Corpus spot
>
> Go through the introduction in the Corpus spot. Then put students in pairs to discuss sentences a–h.
>
> > **Suggested answers**
> > a ? (*totally disinterested* might sound a little strong in some situations)
> > b ✗ (it is not good to call people 'stupid')
> > c ✗ (the language is too critical and should be softened)
> > d ✓
> > e ✗ (the writer could request a refund in a more polite way)
> > f ✓
> > g ✓
> > h ? ('I would be grateful' and 'children' sound better)

5 Encourage students to read the tasks carefully and to have good reasons for making their choice. In Part 2 of the Writing test, students can choose which question to answer and it is very important that they choose a question which they can answer easily (e.g. they may be familiar with the situation, know they have a good range of suitable vocabulary for the topic, etc.). Ask students to plan their answer carefully and to prepare the first draft of the letter. If you would like to highlight one aspect of writing (e.g. connecting words) you could ask students to highlight examples of that feature. Students should write approximately 240 words.

When students exchange their first drafts, encourage constructive criticism and a keen eye for errors. Draw their attention to the Exam information box.

3 In the public eye

GENRE: Interviews
TOPIC: In the media

Speaking	Interviews with famous people
Reading	Interview with Michelle Obama
Listening	Interview with a soap opera star
Grammar	Wishes and regrets
Vocabulary	Idioms (verb + *the* + object)
Speaking	Role play
Workbook contents	
Reading	Supplying questions for answers
Vocabulary	Work vocabulary; *to be at the … of*; suffix *-ee*
Grammar	Wishes and regrets
Listening	Talking about yourself

Student's Book pages 22–25

Lesson planning

SV   Wishes and regrets, exercises 1 or 4; Vocabulary exercises 2 or 4 could be set for homework.

LV   See extension activities in the Speaking 1 and Grammar sections.

Speaking

Extension activity

If you have copies of different kinds of magazines, bring them into the class to generate interest. If a story concerning a famous person has recently broken, you could refer to it and discuss it.

1   Ask students to work in pairs to discuss the questions. Allow time for class feedback, if possible.

Reading

Teaching extra

Prediction exercises help bridge the gap between the classroom and real life. In real life we usually have impressions of people before we really get to know them, or we can have a good guess at the content of an interview. Prediction exercises help students bring this ability or knowledge to their second-language learning.

1   If necessary, give an example of the sort of question we might expect an interviewer to ask Michelle Obama (e.g. *How did you feel when your husband became president of the US?*).

Ask students to predict some other questions the interviewer might ask Michelle Obama. When students have run out of ideas, write their suggestions on the board and leave them there until you have read the text.

2   Ask students to read the interview quickly. Ask them which questions on the board were asked. Even if a question is not the same, if it covers the same topic, tick it off. Then ask students what other questions were asked.

3   Ask students to work in pairs and to discuss their answers and then go through them with the whole class.

Answers

1   A
2   B
3   A
4   B
5   Do you worry that voters can be too easily influenced by election hype?
6   To change things in society you need to work hard and have concrete ideas, not just emotion. Nothing will get done, or expectations may be unrealistic, if we get too emotional.
7   The leader is a person too. People have to change at an individual level if they want to bring about changes in society.

4   Ask students to work with a different partner and discuss questions a–c.

Wishes and regrets

The language here is covered on page 164 of the Grammar folder.

1   In order to establish the grammatical forms which can follow *wish* or *if only*, ask students to complete sentences a–g. If necessary, go through the first sentence as an example.

Possible answers

a had met
b had / had had
c to inform
d were / was
e would brighten up / had brightened up
f wouldn't ask / hadn't asked
g had known

⒠xtension activity

If you would like to spend more time on *wish* or *if only*, write the following headings on the board and go through sentences a–g, completing the table.

	Form	Time reference	Feelings
a	past perfect	past	regret
b	past simple	present/past	a wish for change; regret
c	infinitive	present and future	–
d	unreal past	present	regret
e	*would*	present/future	wish/regret, dissatisfaction, impatience
f	*wouldn't*	present	dissatisfaction, impatience
g	past perfect	past	regret

2   This exercise establishes which structures are possible after *would rather / would prefer*.

Answers
A: <u>Would you prefer to watch</u> an interview with someone, or <u>read</u> it in a magazine?
B: Well, I think <u>I'd prefer to see</u> the person, because when they're asked an awkward question, you can see if <u>they'd prefer not to</u> answer it.
A: I don't like it when people ask awkward questions. For example, why did this interviewer ask about Michelle Obama's personal life?
B: You mean <u>you'd prefer it if she'd focused</u> more on questions about politics?

3   Students complete the sentences.

Answers
a   to have
b   had

4   This exercise could be set for homework. Ask students to quickly read through the whole text first to get the gist of it. Point out that we can say *It's high time ...* and *It's about time ...* to emphasise that something should have been done already.

Answers
1   had / would have   4   had been born
2   read   5   to do
3   woke

5   Encourage students to use the language they have studied in this section.

Listening

1   Ask students to look at the photo and think about the job and say what kind of past they think David Burns might have had. Write up suggestions on the board and generate interest in hearing about this actor.

Leave the suggestions up on the board until you have listened to the interview.

🔊 **1 04** Listen to the interview and then check which topics David Burns talks about. Check what was said against the suggestions on the board.

Answers
school life; a person who helped him; fans, his working relationship with a director; his marriage; his daughter

2   🔊 **1 04** Ask students to listen again for how phrases a–k are used in context. They should try to work out the meaning.

ⓣeaching extra

Promote the habit of deducing meaning from context, which is part of developing learner independence. When students do look words up in a dictionary, encourage them to take note of any multiple meanings (see Unit 2).

3 If practical, after listening, encourage students to walk around the classroom to try to find a student who can help them with some of the words they do not know. Have some English–English dictionaries available for students to check the meanings. Make yourself available if all other means fail.

Answers

a a person in the public eye is written about in newspapers and seen on TV
b a person who hurts or frightens others
c made an unkind remark intentionally to annoy and upset someone
d situation where things go wrong and it feels as if nothing can be done to prevent it
e a difficult childhood
f playing the role of bad people who harm others or break the law
g a nervous/anxious person
h it can become very unpleasant
i unable to stop thinking about something
j I wanted all the public attention for myself
k it's a secret

4 Ask students to discuss the question.

Recording script

Interviewer: With me today in the studio is David Burns, who freely admits that he's had a troubled past. And when I read through this biography – a difficult childhood, married to a fellow soap-opera star, a relationship with a famous actress, an 11-year-old daughter from a subsequent relationship – all I can say, David, is that your life has been a roller coaster. It's no wonder you're constantly in the public eye. Do you think it all started in your teenage years?

David: I think it all stemmed from when I was at school. When I was about 14, I was picked on by a bully. One day, he went too far, saying something about my mother. I snapped. I really laid into him.

Interviewer: What happened?

David: Oh, there was a big fuss at school and I was branded a troublemaker. My mum began to think she couldn't cope with me. Things went from bad to worse. I started avoiding lessons.

Interviewer: And how did you get out of that downward spiral?

David: I was lucky. A drama teacher we had really understood me. She said I could choose to go in whichever direction I wanted. I could continue getting into trouble or I could make something of myself. She was the one who recognised that I had talent.

Interviewer: I wonder if directors see that tough upbringing, because the irony is that you've specialised in playing villains ...

David: I've always been an edgy person. I can bring that out if the part demands it. I've got a dark side. People say they can see an element of that in my eyes.

Interviewer: Does that mean that people think they don't like you as a person, because you always tend to play bad people?

David: Er, I get a very mixed reception. There are fans that write very complimentary letters, saying I'm good-looking and that sort of thing, but then there are those who can't seem to tell fiction from reality, and it can turn nasty.

Interviewer: What do you mean?

David: Well, for example, one fan became obsessed, sort of jealous, and she caused me a lot of problems. She didn't like anyone in the TV series getting near me. She'd send 50 letters every week and pictures from the show with everyone cut out except me. Then she wrote to another cast member saying she knew I had a daughter. That's when I went to my producer, who contacted the police.

Interviewer: Tell us about your experience in *Joseph And The Amazing Technicolor Dreamcoat* ...

David: I played the lead role. I did it for two years – and then I got sacked. The director saw I was getting a lot of attention. I think it was thought I was hogging the limelight. It may have been internal politics, but I wasn't even given the chance to give my final performance.

Interviewer: And tell us about your marriage to your fellow soap-opera star Julia Watts. Do you wish things had worked out better between you?

David: Looking back, I don't think we were destined to spend all our lives together. We just didn't know it at the time. But she's a great actress. She could be in the soap for another 20 years. She's brilliant in it. I've been offered a lot of money to tell my story, but I'm not interested. It's just a pity she's said all those bad things about me in interviews. But if she wants to do that, well, that's her business.

Interviewer: And what about your daughter, Sarah?

David: She's 11 and she's very beautiful and she's talented, too. Her mother, Carol, was a model. When we separated, we always said we'd put Sarah first. She lives with Carol and I see her every other weekend.

Interviewer: Will you ever marry again?

David: I'm in a relationship with someone right now. She's not in show business. But my lips are sealed. I do believe in marriage, but that's all I'll say on the subject.

Vocabulary

Refer students to the Vocabulary spot, focusing on the pattern of the idiom (verb + *the* + object). Point out that, in general, students should look up the verb (e.g. *hog*) in a dictionary.

1   Students can check the answers and meaning with each other, in a dictionary or with you.

> **Answers**
> a 4   b 1   c 6   d 2   e 3   f 5

2   This exercise could be set for homework.

> **Answers**
> 1 test the water   3 called the shots
> 2 delivered the goods 4 saw the light

3   Ask students to work with a partner or in small groups to discuss these questions. The aim is to encourage students to check the meaning of unknown words and phrases, to be more independent and to develop good learning strategies.

4   This exercise could be set for homework.

> **Answers**
> 1 c   2 e   3 a   4 d   5 b

Speaking

1   Go through the Exam spot before starting the Speaking exercise. Students should work with a partner. Make sure that students do not all choose the same famous person.

If your class is quite big, you may prefer to have two interviewers working together and two famous people together. As the students are working on their questions, go round and encourage a variety of question styles. You could write the following types on the board: *direct questions*, *open questions* and *polite questions*. Remind students that they should not mention the interviewee by name because the other students are going to try to guess who is being interviewed.

Set up the role play. Ask students to do their interview in front of the class. You could also either record or video the interviews, telling students that they can vote on the best 'chat show'. Ask students to guess who they think the interviewees are.

To round up, ask the class which interview they liked best.

Exam folder 2

Student's book pages 26–27

Paper 3 Part 2 Open gap fill

Go through the introduction to this task type.

1 and 2 Ask students to first decide what type of word is missing in each gap. They can discuss this in pairs. Then they complete sentences a–j.

Answers
a preposition – *of / in*
b reflexive pronoun – *herself*
c linking device – *whereas / while / but*
d determiner – *every*
e verb – *need*
f relative pronoun – *which / that*
g linking device – *whether / if*
h possessive pronoun – *its*
i part of phrasal verb – *out*
j linking device – *Although / Though*

3 These exercises give students a strategy for dealing with this task type. Possible words that might be gapped in Use of English Part 2 are underlined below. Obviously not all these words would be tested in this text.

Suggested answers
Hollywood actress Kate Beckinsale is <u>never</u> bothered <u>by</u> the hounding paparazzi <u>because</u> she's learned to ignore them.
The *Underworld* actress, <u>who</u> lives in Los Angeles with husband Len Wiseman and her daughter Lily, is <u>in</u> the public eye <u>as</u> soon as she steps out.
<u>However</u>, Beckinsale has <u>her</u> own way of dealing <u>with</u> the intruding paparazzi, and credits her reserved nature <u>for</u> making her ignore the photographers. 'Maybe it's a British thing. I sort of adopt a victim mentality in <u>that</u> I <u>can</u> do <u>nothing</u> about it, <u>so</u> it's pointless throwing things and shouting. I just think, they're going to wait <u>at</u> the bottom of your road and follow you places. Hopefully you're <u>not</u> doing <u>anything</u> so spectacularly interesting <u>like</u> having your pants fall down, because that kind of thing tends to attract attention. It's a part of the job that I tend not to think about that much,' she added.
Beckinsale revealed that even her daughter Lily has adopted her mother's art of ignoring the press. 'It's weird that my daughter's got <u>used</u> to it. We tend to have a group of people following us <u>when</u> we do our Christmas shopping or something but we've all got quite good <u>at</u> blocking it out and pretending it's not happening.'

4 Ask students to look back at the gaps they made. Get feedback from the whole class on their choices.

5 Encourage students to look at the text and discuss the questions, to get the gist of what it is about, without filling in any of the gaps.

Suggested nswers
a 'Jargon' is specialised vocabulary; the 'up side' may refer to the benefits or positive side of jargon.
b Possible examples of jargon in the world of business include 'going forward' or 'driving growth'. Jargon can be useful as a kind of 'shorthand' way of communicating, but it can also exclude people outside the group.

6 and 7 Go through the Exam information box with students, then ask them to complete the task.

Answers
1 relative pronoun – *which / that*
2 personal pronoun – *they*
3 possessive pronoun – *its*
4 part of phrasal verb – *turns*
5 preposition – *for*
6 linking device – *When / Once*
7 pronoun – *something*
8 linking device – *whether*
9 linking device – *when*
10 preposition – *into*
11 preposition – *from*
12 preposition – *of*
13 determiner – *anyone / someone*
14 preposition – *without*
15 personal pronoun – *us*

4 Acting on advice

Listening	Following instructions
Reading	Tips and techniques for improving memory
Grammar	Modals and semi-modals (1)
Listening	Instructions over the phone
Vocabulary	Prefixes and suffixes

Workbook contents

Use of English	Part 1 – multiple-choice gap fill
Listening	Instructions for a recipe
Vocabulary	Prefixes, suffixes, irregular plurals
Grammar	Modals and semi-modals (1)

Student's Book pages 28–31

Lesson planning

SV Modals and semi-modals, exercises 3 and 4 could be set for homework.

LV See extension activities in the Listening and Reading sections.

Listening

1 Use the first question to introduce the unit. Discuss with students how people feel in situations like the ones illustrated in the pictures.

2 🔊 **1 05** Play the recording once and ask students to say what the situation is.

Answer
It's an invigilator giving instructions to candidates at the beginning of an exam.

3

Answer
The imperative form of the verb is used in sentence 1. In sentence 2, a modal verb (*Can you ...?*) is used to front a question.

4 🔊 **1 05** Play the recording again and ask students to identify other phrases used for giving instructions. Point out that imperative forms are common for giving simple, clear instructions but can often sound strict. Modal verbs (e.g. *Can you ...?, Could you ...?, Would you ...?*) are often used to soften instructions and sound more polite.

Suggested answers
Imperatives:
Put your bags at the front of the room.
Only take ...

Conditionals:
If you have ..., please switch it off and leave it in your bag.

Modal verbs:
Please ask if there's ....
Would you mind filling in ...?
Could I ask for ... ?

Recording script
Come into the room quietly and put your bags at the front of the room here. If you have a mobile phone or any other electronic device, please switch if off and leave it in your bag. Only take your pens or pencils to your seat. Can you look for your candidate number on the desk and sit there? That's your place. Good.

Now, I'm going to hand out this form along with the papers. Would you mind filling it in? It's the candidate information sheet. Please ask if there's anything you don't understand.

Right. Could I ask for silence now? I'm going to hand out the papers.

❸xtension activity

Elicit from students what makes good, clear instructions. This can act as a useful link to the next speaking activity.
Good instructions need to be precise, use exact words and the order must be clear. Linking devices are very important. Elicit the type of linking words which would be appropriate (e.g. *Firstly, secondly, then, next, finally, while*).

Good instructions have to bear the listener in mind. If you do not want to appear strict or impolite, it might be better to use modal verbs.

5 Students could work with a partner or in small groups to discuss these questions. Take feedback as a whole-class activity when they have finished.

Reading

1 Ask students to work with a partner and discuss the questions. Leave time for class feedback before going on to the next exercise.

2 Read through the tips and then ask students to discuss which recommendations are most effective and why. Ask students which tips they have tried, or would like to try themselves. This encourages students to give a natural response to the reading, which is what they would do in their own language.

Extension activity

Initiate a discussion on those tips which are particularly useful for language learning. Ask students how they could apply them to learning English.

You could also talk about how students are keeping notes of their language learning, which will be of use for revision before the Advanced exam.

3 Go through the instructions for this activity making sure that everyone understands that Student A reads about technique 1 (the Linkword Technique), Student B reads about technique 2 (the Town Language Mnemonic) and Student C reads about technique 3 (the Hundred Most Common Words). This will lead on to an information-gap activity, so it is important that students only read about their technique.

4 Ask students to create a brief summary of the technique they read about. Students exchange information when they have regrouped. If the majority of students are interested in one of the techniques, try to encourage its use throughout the course.

Modals and semi-modals (1)

The aim here is to draw attention to a range of uses of some common modal verbs. The language here is covered on page 164 of the Grammar folder.

1 Ask students to work with a partner and go through exercise 1.

Answers
a *Could* is used to show that the speaker is requesting action. It shows that the listener has some choice about whether to act in the way the speaker wants.
b *Must* is used here to describe an ideal or desired situation. It is stronger than *should* and shows that the listener has less choice about what to do.
c *Might* is used when making a tentative suggestion – the speaker doesn't want to be too direct or assertive, and wants to give the listener more choice about what to do.

2 Elicit the different meanings of the modal verbs in bold.

Answers
a ability
b making an offer
c negative certainty
d request
e instruction
f theoretical possibility
g permission

3 Ask students to work in pairs and discuss the different uses in each pair.

Answers
1 a The use of *could* suggests a general or physical ability – the person could get into the house by climbing through the window.
  b The use of *was able to* suggests that the person is referring to one specific achievement/occasion.
2 a *may* is used for possibility
  b *May* is used for asking for permission (formal)
3 a *might* is used for possibility (smaller possibility than *may*)
  b *Might* is used for making a suggestion, or tentatively offering advice (formal).
4 a *must* is used for an obligation which comes from the speaker (internal obligation)
  b *have to* is used for an obligation which is imposed on us by someone else (external obligation)
5 a *need* is used to express the idea that it is necessary to do something.
  b *didn't need to* is used when someone has done something, but it wasn't necessary to do it.
6 a *needn't have* is used to tell someone that an action they did wasn't necessary.
  b *don't need to* is used to say that an action is not necessary.

4 You might like students to work in pairs and prepare this writing task in class first. Alternatively, you could set it for homework. Encourage students to choose a subject which they find interesting.

5 Point out the perfect form *might have* + past participle and the continuous form *might be* + -*ing*. Go through the example which relates to the pictures and elicit other possibilities from students.

Suggested answers
A He might have been caught in the rain.
B She might have fallen over.
C They might have just had an accident.
D She might be doing her homework.
E They might have got lost.

Listening

1   **1 06** As a lead-in, elicit students' experiences of talking to recorded messages when they phone a company. Then listen to the recording and go through each of the questions.

Answers
a press 1
b press 2
c press 2
d press 4
e your flight confirmation number and some form of identification with a photograph on it
f call 0800 952 43 43 or visit the website at www.askstl.net
g press 2 to speak to the fault management centre
h press 4

Recording script

Message 1: Thank you for calling the Booking Information Service. If you wish to purchase tickets for *Avatar 3*, please press 1. If you wish to see *Love in New York*, please press 2. If you'd like information about times and prices, please press 3. If you would like to speak to one of our staff, press the star key.

Message 2: Thank you for calling FlyHappy, Europe's best low-cost airline. Please select one of the four following options. For timetable information, please press 1. If you wish to make a booking, press 2. For general enquiries, press 3. Or to book one of our fantastic last-minute promotional offers, press 4. If you would like to speak to one of our agents, please hold the line and a FlyHappy agent will be with you shortly. Please note that FlyHappy is now a ticketless airline. In order to check in, all you need is your flight confirmation number and a form of photo ID. Thank you for calling FlyHappy.

Message 3: Hi, thanks for calling STL. Please listen carefully to the following options which are designed to help us assist you with your call. If your call is regarding information for our exciting new internet service, STL Netclub, please call our exclusive hotline number on 0800 952 43 43, that's 0800 952 43 43. Alternatively, visit our website at www.askstl.net. If you would like to make a payment by credit or debit card, please press 1. If you need to report a fault, please press 2 to speak to our customer assistance centre. If you have an enquiry about an existing account and would like to speak to a representative, please press 3. If you are not an existing customer and would like information about the services we offer, please press 4. For all other enquiries, please hold while we transfer you to a customer service representative.

2   Generate discussion on this topic, according to how interested your students are.

Vocabulary

Teaching extra

In Part 3 of the Use of English test (Paper 3), the words which candidates have most difficulty with are often those which require them to add a prefix or suffix. In many cases, this may be because candidates have not read the text for meaning.

1   Refer students to the Exam spot, then go through the introduction with the class.

Ask students to work with a partner and put the words under the correct headings. Check the meaning of any unknown words before students do the exercise. Sometimes, you need to add a hyphen when you add a prefix (e.g. *non-smoker*). Tell students that it is best to check in a dictionary if they are not sure.

Answers
dis- disappear, discontinue, distrust
non- non-smoker
il- illogical, illiterate
mis- mislead, mistrust
im- immature, immaterial, impolite
un- unbelievable, untimely, unexpected
in- inaccessible, insensitive, inconclusive
ir- irrational, irregular

2   Use the table to elicit the rules for the use of *im-*, *il-* and *ir-*.

Answers
a *im-*   b *il-*   c *ir-*

3   Go through the Vocabulary spot on suffixes and prefixes with the class. Ask students to work with a partner and put the words under the correct heading. Check the meaning of the words before students do the exercise.

Answers
(The words in bold show where the spelling of the original word has changed.)
-able: photocopiable, countable, employable, **arguable**, recommendable, respectable, **reliable**
-ation: emancipation, **dramatisation**, recommendation
-ency: efficiency, **frequency**, **tendency**
-ful: deceitful, careful, respectful
-ly: timely, rudely, frequently, calmly
-less: countless, timeless, speechless, careless, pointless
-ment: judg(e)ment, employment, **argument**
-ness: rudeness, calmness

Writing folder 2

Formal writing

1 Go through the two introductory sentences to point out the difference between formal and informal language.

Suggested answers
Give us a ring soon is informal English, probably spoken and used with someone who the speaker knows well.
We look forward to hearing from you at your earliest convenience is formal English, almost certainly written and probably used with someone the speaker does not know well.

2 It is impossible to be absolutely precise about the ordering of these but they are likely to be in the following order (from the most formal to the least formal).

Suggested answers
1 proposal to a benefactor on how you would spend the money he might give you
2 report for your boss
3 contribution to a tourist guidebook
4 letter of complaint to a newspaper
5 leaflet for a local sports club
6 competition entry for an international magazine
7 review for an English Club newsletter
8 article for a student magazine
9 email to a pen friend

3 Ask students to read through the advice. With a partner, they should then modify the pieces of advice if necessary to make them more appropriate.

Suggested answers
a It is not usually appropriate to use verb contractions in formal writing.
b Try to avoid phrasal verbs in formal writing, although sometimes there is no alternative or the alternative would sound too stilted to be appropriate.
c Avoid slang or colloquial expressions in formal writing – if they are included, it will be done for some special effect.
d Layout is more fixed in formal contexts.
e Structure is always important, but because you are more likely to be writing formally to someone you do not know and with whom you do not have so much shared knowledge, clarity of structure is particularly important.
f Again, this is important in all kinds of writing but may perhaps be particularly so in formal writing (as one way of clarifying structure).

4 Encourage students to use a wide variety of interesting and appropriate adjectives. Point out that any word suggested as a replacement for *nice*, *good* or *beautiful* will add something extra and different to the meaning of the sentence.

Answers
a lovely, fascinating   d varied
b stimulating, talented   e friendly; impressive
c sumptuous; spectacular

Corpus spot

Go through the Corpus spot introduction with students. Put them in pairs and ask them to rewrite each sentence. Point out that the sentences are all grammatically correct but could be improved stylistically. Get feedback from the whole class.

Suggested answers
a Moreover, we are content with your staff. Having kind and helpful personnel is important – people expect this ~~kind of stuff~~ **level of service**.
b Lastly, I would like to say that the discount seems ~~a bit~~ **rather / slightly** smaller than the ten per cent originally promised.
c I am writing this letter to your newspaper because I think ~~you guys made~~ **there was** a mistake **in your Thursday edition** ~~the other day~~.
d Interviewees' responses depended on ~~how old they were, whether they were male or female,~~ **their age, gender, occupation and educational background.**
e ~~And some more things~~ **With regard to other matters**, I would like to make a few suggestions, which I hope you can take into consideration.

5 The three texts provide further practice in using connecting words. Remind students to read through each text as a whole before filling in the gaps.

Answers
1 Firstly	5 Although	9 then
2 Secondly	6 So	10 Firstly
3 Moreover	7 However	11 when
4 Finally	8 Consequently	12 Gradually
		13 After that
		14 especially
		15 because
		16 Finally

6 Students can prepare this writing task in class or it could be set for homework if time is short. Encourage students to bear in mind all the work they have just done on formal writing.

5 Dear Sir or Madam

GENRE: Formal writing
TOPIC: Dream jobs

Speaking	Formal writing
Reading	The secrets of formal writing
Writing	A job application
Vocabulary	Connotation
Grammar	Relative clauses
Listening	Interview with a Formula One driver

Workbook contents

Grammar	Relative clauses
Vocabulary	Connotation
Writing	A formal letter
Use of English	Part 1 – multiple-choice gap fill

Student's Book pages 34–37

Lesson planning

SV Writing exercise 2d and Vocabulary exercise 4 could be set for homework.

LV See the extension activity in the Speaking section.

Speaking

1 Answers to these question may depend on the age and nationality of your students.

Suggested answers
a Letters of complaint, application letter, etc. To managers, customers, etc.
b It can be difficult to write formal messages because you have to think about the effect you want to have on the person who receives the message. You have to choose your language carefully. Informal messages may be easier, especially if they are for friends (you can use abbreviations, emoticons, less specific language, etc.).

2 Ask students to read the extracts from formal letters and to decide on the purpose of each letter. Draw attention to formal set phrases (e.g. *on behalf of ...*) and formal vocabulary (e.g. *commence*).

Answers
a to express sympathy for a person's ill health (*We all hope you get well soon!*)
b to apologise for an awkward situation (*We're so sorry for all the trouble we've caused.*)
c to remind someone about an unpaid invoice (*I don't think you've paid – could you check?*)
d to offer someone employment (*Write and let us know if you're interested in this offer, and when you can start work.*)
e to introduce a colleague (*Ms Wright is working on a project you might be interested in. She'll be in touch with you soon about a meeting.*)
f to request information (*Please send the details of the Nile Cruise. Thanks.*)

3

Suggested answer
The purpose of the letter is to complain. No one from the hotel has contacted Dr Robertson about the items which disappeared from his hotel room. The hotel promised that they would let him know the outcome of the reported loss. Dr Robertson also wants to point out that until he has heard from the hotel, he cannot proceed with his insurance claim.

4

Answers
a at the end
b *Yours sincerely*
c 1 *articles* 2 *upon our discovering it* 3 *in turn* 4 *as* 5 *as yet* 6 *regarding*
d *I'm looking forward to*

Extension activity

Students plan and write a brief reply to Dr Robertson on behalf of the hotel, apologising and explaining what happened.

Reading

1   You could brainstorm the 'secrets' of formal writing as a whole class first, writing students' suggestions up on the board. Then ask students to work with a partner and to match the headings with the 'secrets'.

> **Answers**
> a 5   b 7   c 2   d 3   e 6   f 1   g 4

2   Ask students to work in pairs to discuss the secrets.

Writing

1   **1 07** Tell students to imagine that a friend has just told them he's got a dream job. Ask them what might be a dream job for a young man who loves sport and travel and is interested in ecology. Then tell them to listen to find out and to answer the questions.

> **Answers**
> a   Caretaker of the Islands of the Great Barrier Reef
> b   A$150,000, that's US$103,000, or £70,000 for six months and a rent-free three-bedroom villa, complete with pool.

Recording script

Leo: Look at this advert.

Silvia: What is it?

Leo: They want someone to be the 'Caretaker of the Islands of the Great Barrier Reef'. It's a completely new job.

Silvia: What would you have to do?

Leo: Just live on a beautiful island for six months and watch the fish swim by!

Silvia: I can't believe that's for real. It sounds like a holiday!

Leo: Well, there's more to it than that. The Great Barrier Reef is a World Heritage Listed natural wonder – and the islands of the Great Barrier Reef have, it says here, an 'abundance' of wildlife, so it's an important site for naturalists. This sounds just my thing. It says the Island Caretaker will be based on Hamilton Island – that's the largest inhabited island in the region.

Silvia: So if that's off the coast of Queensland, it'll be warm all year round and then there'll be the blue skies, crystal-clear waters and … What's the catch?

Leo: No formal qualifications needed but ideal candidate must be able to swim, snorkel, dive, sail … I can do all that. The successful applicant will receive a salary of A$150,000 – not bad – for six months and get to live rent-free in a three-bedroom villa, complete with pool. Wow!

Silvia: What are you waiting for? Who you do have to write to?

---

2   Go through the Exam spot and point out that in the Writing test (Paper 2), students may be asked to write an informal and/or formal letter, so it is very important that they can distinguish between the two. Remind students of their discussions in the Speaking section. Before students plan the letter of application for the job in Australia, play the recording again and tell students to note down what skills are needed for the job. They should then discuss what sort of background and personal qualities the caretaker will need.

> **Possible answers**
> interested in marine life, self-reliant, able to self-motivate, able to use initiative, well organised and self-disciplined

Students plan the letter of application with a partner. They could compare plans and decide on the best ideas.

Ask students to write the first draft of the letter in pairs. Monitor them as they work, checking layout, punctuation and language. Then, students swap first drafts with another pair. Finally, students write the final draft in class if time permits, so that a good final version is produced which can then be kept as an example. Alternatively, this could be set for homework.

Vocabulary

Go through the Vocabulary spot with students to make sure that they understand the concept of connotation.

1   Ask students to work in pairs to do the exercise.

> **Possible answers**
> a   I have successfully completed a first-aid course.
> b   I can speak English fluently. (Or indicate the correct level or course attended.)
> c   I am able attend an interview at your earliest convenience.
> d   I am willing to work shifts.
> e   I have excellent communication skills.

2   This exercise shows how certain words can be inappropriate in certain situations because of their connotation, even though they may be grammatically correct, or the meaning is generally understood.

3 Ask students to work with a partner to find an equivalent for each word or phrase.

4 This exercise could be set for homework.

Relative clauses

Most students at this level will have studied relative clauses before but the omission of the relative pronoun and the position of prepositions provide advanced practice. The language here is covered on page 165 of the Grammar folder.

1 Use these sentences as a diagnostic tool to assess your students' knowledge of these structures.

2 Ask students to work with a partner if they find this exercise difficult.

3 Elicit from students that we can leave out the relative pronoun when it is the object of its clause.

4 This exercise could be set for homework.

5 Point out that in more formal English, we tend to put the preposition before the relative pronoun, instead of at the end of the sentence. We use which not that, to refer to things. We use whom, not who/that to refer to people when they are the object of the main clause.

6 Go through the Corpus spot before the exercise. Then ask students to rewrite the sentences in formal style, paying particular attention to the position of the prepositions.

Listening

1 The aim of the pre-listening questions is to get students thinking about the topic and to make the interview more interesting and accessible. After students have had enough time for their discussion, get some class feedback. Then go through the Exam spot and explain that sentence completion is one of the task types in the Listening test (Paper 4).

2 Ask students to try to predict possible words which could fill the gaps.

3 **1 08** Play the recording once and then ask the students to compare their answers. Play the recording again and remind students to check that the whole sentence makes grammatical sense.

Answers
a a camera crew	e sponsors
b calm	f boat
c sixth	g university
d petrol	

Recording script

Interviewer: The darkness refuses to lift over the racetrack and the clouds are hanging over the motor home. A tiny race suit is hanging in the corner, but the young man sitting on the sofa is not ready for it yet as he rubs his eyes and comes to terms with the fact that he could still be snuggled up in bed instead of putting himself on display – yet again – at such an unearthly hour. Cesar, how did you get yourself into this business?

Cesar: Well, it's all down to my coach. He took a calculated risk with me when I was completely unknown. And then, as you know, it was a rapid change for me as I suddenly became famous.

Interviewer: How has your family coped with your fame and, I suppose, their fame too?

Cesar: Well, the fame thing doesn't bother me, most people don't disturb me when they see me eating in a restaurant or something like that but I think my mother finds it a bit disturbing, you know, having to deal with a camera crew every time she comes out of the house. And in fact, my sisters now, they don't come down to the track to see me race, they watch me on TV at home.

Interviewer: Your father has shown great faith in you, hasn't he?

Cesar: Well, I think both of us have had many doubts at times about my talent but he reckons it's being calm which makes the difference between champions and the rest. He's amazing too – he's become really hardened to the constant attention. And he's the one who has to watch from the sidelines. I think that must be a lot worse than doing the race.

Interviewer: Yes, you had a scary moment in Australia, didn't you?

Cesar: Yeah, I'd qualified the twenty-first and in the race got up to sixth position before my car gave out. It was really scary. You've only got split seconds to make life and death decisions. I knew straightaway something had gone wrong with the car and then you've got to get off the track and out of the way of the other drivers as fast as you can.

Interviewer: And you did it. But from an early age you proved that you've got what it takes.

Cesar: Oh, I don't know. When I left school as a teenager it was just hard work. I went from track to track. And, yeah, I suppose when I had to live in Italy and Belgium on my own it was a bit tough, but my dad was a great support. I remember he had to borrow money so that I could afford petrol, just to get to a race once. And that's only a couple of years ago.

Interviewer: Things are very different now – you've got sponsors queuing up to take you on and make you a millionaire.

Cesar: And I've already got more money than I'd ever dreamed of but I'm trying to be sensible with the money.

Interviewer: I've heard about the Ferrari in the garage and the BMW sports car. What's next on the list?

Cesar: I'm not irresponsible, even though to many people it must seem like I am. But it's strange what money and fame can do to you. I mean, it just seems normal to me now to have all those things and, in fact, if I had to say, I would like a boat. I'd love that, to have it somewhere hot.

Interviewer: Does this mean that you have nothing or little in common with your old friends back home?

Cesar: When I go back home I still meet up with my old friends but lots of them have moved on too, they're living in different places, or they have new family lives, so I don't get to see them so often. I suppose at our age, people are moving around a lot and doing different things. I don't think my situation is any different. It's just that I've changed jobs. But when we meet up we still talk about the same things. Like we never changed.

Interviewer: He might not have changed among his friends, but on Sunday he will be the new young star of Formula One, driving in front of five hundred million TV viewers.

4 Round off the Listening section with a class discussion.

Units 1–5 Revision

Student's book pages 38–39

Topic review

Ask students to work with a partner to discuss questions a–i. The aim of this exercise is to encourage students to recycle the vocabulary and structures they have covered in the preceding units in a personalised way.

Grammar

1   If you think your students will need more guidance to complete the text, you could give them the root of the verb required.

Answers
1   could
2   hadn't come / wasn't / weren't
3   go / we went
4   could have come / had come / were
5   grew
6   had come / were

Vocabulary

1   When checking the answers, check that students have understood what type of word is required.

Answers
1 D   2 B   3 C   4 D   5 C   6 B   7 C   8 A
9 C   10 D

2   Ask students to work with a partner. Make English–English dictionaries available if possible.

Suggested answers
a   sit / take; pass; fail
b   enter
c   make up; changed; speaks
d   wide / great / huge
e   make

3   Ask students to complete the sentences with an appropriate word formed with a prefix or suffix.

Answers
a   misled
b   shatterproof
c   popularity
d   boyhood
e   underdone
f   reclaim
g   impolite

4

Possible answers
a   she got a reply – she received a reply/response
        at a time that is good for you – at your convenience
    I'm looking forward to – I look forward to
    but – however,
    a job like that – a similar job
        I'm writing about the advert in ... – I am writing
    regarding / in connection with the advertisement in ...
    I'm always on time – I am punctual
    I'd like the chance to – I would welcome the
        opportunity
b   consider – think about
    discuss – talk about
    a great deal of – a lot
    to commence – to start
    Please accept my sincerest apologies – I'm sorry
    to purchase – to buy
    I wish you a speedy recovery – Get well soon
    to exceed a word limit – to go over a word limit
    please circulate this email to – please send this email to
        everyone
    to ensure – to make sure

5

Answers
1   by
2   to
3   in
4   when / if
5   through
6   which
7   across
8   like
9   who
10   up
11   for
12   off
13   into
14   for
15   with

6 Connections

GENRE: Phone messages
TOPIC: Communications technology

Speaking	Telephone technology
Grammar	Phrasal verbs (1)
Speaking	Phrasal verbs
Vocabulary	Collocations (*have, do, make* and *take*)
Reading	The Joys of Texting
Workbook contents	
Listening	Note completion
Grammar	Phrasal verbs
Vocabulary	Collocations (*do, have, make, take*)

Student's book pages 40–43

Lesson planning
SV   Grammar exercise 3 could be set for homework.
LV   See the extension activity in the Vocabulary section.

Speaking

1   Ask students to discuss these introductory questions in pairs or small groups. Allow time for feedback relating to each of the questions.

Some telephone services may not be universally familiar:

- internet phone (e.g. Skype or Nonoh) is a way of talking to someone via the internet. If you both have a webcam then you can see each other as well as hear each other.
- voicemail is an electronic message-taking service used by businesses.
- apps are software applications (e.g. an app might tell you what the time is in any place in the world or what the traffic is like in the area you are interested in).
- texting is sending written messages from one mobile phone to another.
- a ring-back service helps if you are ringing someone who is engaged. It makes an automatic connection for you when the person you are trying to contact puts the phone down.
- the speaking clock is a telephone service in the UK which states the precise time when dialled.

2 **1 09** Ask students to read through the questions, then play the recording once. Students should compare their answers in pairs.

Suggested answers
a Her boyfriend had decided he had got tired of her and wanted to end their relationship.
b She dialled an automatic recorded message from his phone while he was away for a month and then left the phone off the hook.
c students' own answers

Recording script
Oh, talking of revenge, I read about a great one once. There was this woman, she'd been dumped by her boyfriend, 'cos he'd decided he'd gone off her and he told her to move her things out of his flat before he got back from a business trip. I think he was going to the States for a month or something. Anyway, she moves her stuff out straightaway but before she leaves, she picks up the phone and dials the speaking clock. Then she leaves the phone off the hook while the clock goes on telling the time to an empty flat. 'At the third stroke, it'll be 10.25 and 30 seconds …' So the boyfriend finds it when he returns four weeks later. You can imagine what the bill was like after a solid month of this. Huge! That must have been really satisfying for the dumped woman!

Phrasal verbs (1)

1 **1 10** Play the messages all the way through once and ask students to take down as much information as they can. Play the recording again message-by-message for students to complete the information and then check their answers.

Answers
1 **For:** Andy
From: Eddie
Number: 07930 245 908
Message: What was website? Please ring back before two (has to go to seminar).

2 For: Michael Removals
From: Robert Smith
Number: 0207 562 495
Message: Recommended by Richard Johnstone. Wants to know charges for moving a few things on 22nd or 21st. Is moving beds, chests of drawers, fridge, washing machine, etc. out of house (moving about one mile). Also could you fix in the washing machine for him?

3 For: Nicky
From: Leila
Number: not given
Message: Just wants a gossip. (Jo's resigned – wants to tell you why!)

4 For: Nicola
From: Olga
Number: not given
Message: Calling from Omsk. Not back till 19th (has to do extra workshop). Will get bus home from airport – flight gets in 10.15 so should be home by midday. May try calling again later.

5 For: Piotr
From: Jens
Number: not given
Message: Leaving party tonight meeting in the King's Pub next to the station, 6:30 NOT 7:30.

6 For: Matt
From: Alex
Number: not given
Message: Has new game. Do you want to go round and play it?

2 ▸1 10 Play the recording again. You could give students a photocopy of the recording script on this page.
Ask them to highlight the phrasal verbs in the script. Write them on the board. Note that some of them are repeated in several conversations. Point out that there is quite a high concentration of phrasal verbs because the English used is fairly informal spoken English, where phrasal verbs are typical.

Answers
a look up; ring me back; show up; call back; fix those in; get back; catch up; give me a ring; fill you in; get through; cut off; put me through; gets in; run out; Hang on; come round; break up; hang up
b 1 break up 2 put through to 3 hang on 4 hang up 5 get through to 6 cut off

3 Students work through the exercise individually or in pairs.

Answers
a your coins run out
b get through
c them to speak up
d put you through
e Hang on a moment.
f pass you over

Recording script
Recording script

Speaker 1: Hi, Andy. I wanted to know about our homework. This history project. What was that website you said I should look up? I hope we can type it. Can you ring me back? Oh, this is Eddie by the way, I don't think I said. In case my number isn't showing up on your phone, it's 07930 245 908. I've got my seminar at two, so if you can call back before then, great. Bye.

Speaker 2: Hello, is that Michael Removals? Richard Johnstone gave me your number and suggested I contact you. I was wondering if you could move some stuff on the 21st or 22nd. It's just some beds and chests of drawers and bits and pieces into a house. I'm only moving about a mile away. Oh yes, and there's a fridge, and a washing machine too. Would you be able to fix those in for me as well, to the new place? Could you get back to me and let me know your charges? My name's Robert Smith, on 0207 562 495.

Speaker 3: Hi Nicky, it's Leila. Just ringing for a bit of a catch up of the latest gossip. There's some news you might be interested in. Jo's decided to resign. And wait until you hear why. There'll soon be nobody left at all here. Anyway, give me a ring when you can and I'll fill you in on all the details. Bye.

Speaker 4: Hi Nicola, It's Olga. I'm calling from Omsk, and it's taken me ages to get through to you. Are you OK? I tried ringing you at work a couple of times but kept getting cut off before they could put me through to you. Anyway, I just wanted to let you know that I won't be back till the 19th. They want me to do an extra workshop on the 18th and they've managed to rearrange my flights for me. Don't worry about meeting me. I'll just catch the bus home from the airport. The flight gets in at 10.15, so I'll probably be home after midday. OK, I'm going to try calling again later. Bye.

Speaker 5: Hi Piotr, it's Jens. I left my mobile at home so I'm calling from the street. Haven't used one of these for ages so hope I can tell you everything before my coins run out. OK. So we're meeting for the leaving party at 6:30 tonight not 7:30. Hang on a moment. I'll just find the address. Yes, here it is. It's the King's Pub next to the station. OK, see you there later. Bye.

Speaker 6: Matt? This is Alex. I've downloaded version two. The graphics are just amazing. Do you want to come round and play it? I've got to get my homework done first but that'll only take ten minutes. I'll ... Oh – I think I'm breaking up. I'm going to hang up. I'll text you.

Speaking

1 Ask students to match the two parts of the dialogues, then check the answers together. To get students practising more, ask them to improvise and extend each dialogue for up to one minute.

Vocabulary

1 Check that all students are clear about the concept of collocation (words that are frequently used together). Students can work individually or with a partner on this exercise. Suggest that they do the ones they are sure about first and leave the rest for the moment. When they have done all the ones they are sure about, check the answers as a class. Then suggest students use dictionaries to deal with any remaining items (if necessary).

Go through the Corpus spot with students. Point out that this type of mistake with collocations is very common among learners.

Corpus spot

Extension activity

As homework, students prepare more sentences with gaps using some of the collocations they have been working with. These can then be used by other students in the class as a follow-up or revision of the collocations practised in this section.

Reading

This reading text has been labelled with a C2 icon. This corresponds with the C2 ('Mastery') level of the *Common European Framework of Reference for Languages*.

Candidates who can demonstrate language ability at a C1 level receive a grade B or C in the Cambridge English: Advanced exam. Exceptional candidates, who demonstrate ability at a C2 level, receive a grade A.

Text and language marked with the C2 icon have been developed to include coverage of the requirements of the C2 level, helping students to improve their general degree of skill and also demonstrating the kind of level that C2 reaches.

1 You might want to point out to students that this is a more difficult text than usual. The writer demonstrates a particularly playful use of English, using irony and satire. Rather than pointing out facts, the writer is offering a particular opinion, and students will have to read 'between the lines' to understand what that opinion is. Ask students to look through the text quickly to get a general sense of what it is about, and then to answer the questions.

2   Ask students to discuss the questions with a partner.
    Take feedback on any items that caused discussion.

> **Answers**
> a texting
> b texting for long periods
> c a Museum of Texting
> d the invention of the 'Immobile Phone'
> e person-to-person conversation
> f phone-free conversation

3   Students discuss their answers in pairs. Then discuss
    suggestions with the class as a whole.

> **Suggested answers**
> *come out* (*wrong*) = were typed inaccurately
> *came out* (*right*) = were typed accurately
> *leave out* (*all the vowels*) = omit
> *texted back* = responded
> (*message had*) *got through* = reached its destination
> *drawn out* = extended
> *dress up* = wear fancy dress
> *came up with* (*the bright idea*) = had
> (*battery*) *running down* = losing its charge
> *walking around* = walking (the around is not strictly
>   necessary)
> *switch off* = unwind
> *come up with* (*a way*) = devised
> (*PFC has*) *taken off* = become a great success

4   Find the answers with the class as a whole.

> **Answers**
> **take** time
> **have** no way (of knowing)
> **reach** a destination
> **take** place
> **come up** with a (bright) idea
> **come up** with a way of
> **set** one's mind to
> **have** no idea (*PFC has*) *taken off* = become a great success

5   Focus students on the photos. They discuss their ideas
    in groups of three or four. Round up with the whole
    class when everyone has finished.

Exam folder 3

Student's book pages 44–45
Paper 3 Part 3 Word formation

This section aims to help students cope with Part 3 of the Use of English test (Paper 3).

1 and 2 The parts of speech are provided in brackets below together with the words that were originally in the text. Although it should be possible to identify the required part of speech, it is unlikely that students will identify all the original words and several alternatives may be equally possible. Accept any likely alternatives.

Answers
1 (adverb) *viciously*
2 (adjective) *courteous*
3 (noun) *team*
4 (verb–past tense) *ordered*
5 (noun) *union*
6 (adjective) *unruly*
7 (verb–past participle) *saved*
8 (noun–plural) *pupils*

3 Ask students to think back to the work done on prefixes in Unit 4.

Answers

Verbs	Adjectives	Nouns
unwrap	unsafe	disappearance
de-ice	disloyal	insecurity
misspell	insane	unease
untie	uncomfortable	discomfort
disentangle	non-European	immobility
misunderstand	irresponsible	imbalance

Corpus spot

Answers
a ~~unsatisfaction~~ dissatisfation
b ~~dissatisfactory~~ unsatisfactory
c ~~unadequate~~ inadequate
d ~~unorganised~~ disorganised
e ~~unexpensive~~ inexpensive

4 You may wish to add other words to the list in addition to those suggested.

Possible answers
law: lawyer, lawful, unlawful, lawless, law-abiding
hope: hopeful, hopeless, hopelessness, hopefully
act: action, actor, react, reaction, enact, enactment
press: pressure, pressing, depress, oppress, repress, oppression, oppressive, oppressor
centre: central, centrally, centralise, decentralise, centralisation, concentrate, concentration
head: heading, header, subhead, behead, heady, big-headed, pig-headed
office: officer, official, officiate, officious, officially
broad: breadth, broaden, broadly, broad-minded

5 This exercise is similar to the one students will need to do in the exam.

Answers
1 inspection
2 violence
3 leadership
4 outrageous
5 uncontrollable / uncontrolled
6 later
7 properly
8 councillors
9 successful
10 unsatisfactory
11 remarkably

6 This provides further practice of the exam task.

Answers

1 happily	8 discharged
2 skilled	9 convulsions
3 recognition	10 psychological
4 unfamiliar	11 limitations / limits
5 injury	12 marriage
6 dislodged	13 fortunately
7 safety	

Teaching extra

Ask students to find at least one other word based on the same root for each of the root words in exercise 5 or 6. They could then write sentences with blanks to test their words. For example, *Harry took a degree in accounting and then became a tax _____.* (*INSPECT*)
Students then test each other with their sentences.

A successful business

GENRE: Reports
TOPIC: The world of work

Speaking	Work and business
Reading	A successful young entrepreneur
Vocabulary	Multiple meanings and word formation
Grammar	Reason, result and purpose
Writing	Reports
Listening and speaking	People and their jobs

Workbook contents

Reading	True/False exercise
Grammar	Reason, result and purpose
Use of English	Part 1 – multiple-choice gap fill

Student's book pages 46–49

Lesson planning

SV Reading exercise 3 and Writing exercises 1 or 2 could be set for homework.

LV See extension activities in the Vocabulary and Listening and speaking sections.

Speaking

1 Ask students to discuss these questions in small groups to arouse their interest in the topic.

Reading

1 Allow students enough time to read the article quickly without worrying about what words might fill the gaps. Then ask them questions a–d.

Answers
a 13
b scooters
c family and friends
d companies were happy to give him advice

Teaching extra

This exercise helps to train students in the skills needed to do Part 2 of the Use of English paper. Questions a–d show that it is possible, indeed necessary, to understand what the text is about before filling in the gaps. Use this procedure whenever you are working with a similar exercise type in class. Encourage students to read the text through first, check their comprehension by asking a few comprehension questions and only then begin to think about how to fill the gaps in the text.

2 Encourage students to look at the words on either side of each gap to help them.

Answers

1	in	8	in
2	up	9	needed
3	one	10	in, during
4	neither / nor	11	them
5	if	12	in
6	which	13	do, did
7	did, sold	14	what

3 Students should do the exercise, then discuss their answers with a partner.

Answers
1 B   2 B   3 C   4 B

Vocabulary

1 Students should work on this exercise individually or in pairs. Point out that all the words are to be found in the reading article and can be found in the order in which they come in the exercise.

Answers

1	market	4	break
2	company	5	exploded
3	boot	6	presentation

2 Deal with this exercise as a class. Again, all the words are to be found in the reading text and are used in the order in which they come in the exercise.

Answers

1	freedom	4	competitors
2	presenter	5	explosive
3	variety	6	childish

Reason, result and purpose

The language here is covered on page 166 of the Grammar folder.

1   Read the article and discuss the question with the class as a whole.

> **Answers**
> a   *be a consequence of ...*
> b   *in order to get ...*
> c   *because of ...*

2   You could go through the Corpus spot before asking students to do exercise 2. Ask students to do the exercise individually and then compare their answers with those of a partner.

> **Answers**
> 1   so
> 2   because
> 3   Having had
> 4   so
> 5   so as to
> 6   because of
> 7   As a result of
> 8   with the result that

3   Students discuss the idea of 'success'. Get feedback from the whole class.

Writing

1   Students might be expected to write such a report in Part 1 of the Writing test (Paper 2), although at over 500 words, this one is longer than any report they would be required to write in the exam. They should, therefore, pay careful attention to all aspects of its structure and language.

> **Answers**
> The report is generally positive.

2   Ask students to think about the questions as they read the report. They can discuss answers with a partner. Questions b and c may be set for homework.

> **Suggested answers**
> a   The headings are appropriate and useful in that they state clearly what each paragraph includes. The report is clear and unambiguous and uses headings to inform and guide the reader. The report therefore follows a fairly standard pattern.
> b   Some students may feel that some other words and expressions also have a linking function in the text (e.g. *there, in a number of ways*, etc.). Allow anything to be included that students can justify. However, make sure that the phrases listed below are highlighted and discussed by all the class. Ask students what the function is of each of the words and phrases in the box.
> *Firstly, Secondly, Thirdly, Finally* – listing points
> *Moreover* – adding a point
> *For example* – giving an example
> *In conclusion* – drawing a conclusion
> *However* – making a point that contrasts in some way with what has gone before
> c   *thanks to, as a result of, Consequently, this has led us*

3   Compare students' ideas for headings and discuss what might be included under the headings suggested.

Listening and Speaking

1   Brainstorm ideas and write them on the board.

2   **1 11** Ask students to listen to the recording and answer questions a–c.

> **Answers**
> 1   hairdresser
> 2   private detective
> 3   stunt woman
> 4   window cleaner
> 5   fitness instructor
> 6   journalist
> 7   psychologist
> 8   sports commentator

Recording script

Speaker 1: When I was at school, I decided I definitely wanted a career and I thought about what I could do working with other people. I got a part-time job in a salon, and it was not until I got an apprenticeship that I really thought this is what I want to do. I love the work because you meet different people every day. You can be creative, which is important to me. If there is any downside, it's that you're on your feet all day, but at the end of the day, it's something I really love doing.

Speaker 2: Well, this job found me, really. A friend recommended me and so I did a job for someone and it seemed to work out OK. I never fancied doing a run-of-the-mill job, nine-to-five, and I quite like the secrecy of what I'm doing now. There is a lot of boring paper work – it's not as dramatic as you see in the films – but the best part is when I'm out on the street. I'm a private man by nature, so it sort of suits me.

Speaker 3: Initially, I wanted to be an actor and then I realised, eventually, that wasn't going to happen. I've always been sporty and I used to go to judo class every week, and then got more and more interested, and sort of started going more often. It was my teacher who sort of suggested I get into it. So he introduced me to someone, and I've been on film sets ever since, really. There's a lot of travel, which sometimes gets me down, but I do get to meet famous people – including the ones I'm supposed to be.

Speaker 4: I got into it by accident really. I needed extra money, and I've always liked, you know, the outdoors and getting out and all that sort of thing, so I just decided to give it a try and keep on going. It's not been bad – lucrative even. And it's hard work. It's harder work than you imagine, especially when you're out in the cold. You've got to have a head for heights, too. The nice thing is the satisfaction on people's faces, looking at people's faces afterwards when they realise they can actually see outside again.

Speaker 5: I'd always been interested in fitness. I was, actually, a gym champion when I was young. Then I decided what to do when I grew up and, yeah, it was, it was a really good choice in the end because what I really like is helping other people get fit, and to actually bring out the best in them. I can advise them what to do and what not to do, what's best for their muscles and, yeah, it's really worthwhile.

Speaker 6: First of all, well, I did an English degree and then I didn't know what to do really, after that. I wanted to get out and, you know, do a job where you sort of meet a lot of people and so I fell into it, really. It's great, you know, because you meet a lot of interesting people. What I really like about it is you're always breaking a story, so whatever you get involved in is, you know, always going to be interesting. I suppose the thing I don't like is the public's perception of us as being like the paparazzi, never reporting the truth, always up to no good. But I think we do a very important job. If someone's famous, then it's in the public interest to sort of find out as much as possible about them, you know, and that's what I do.

Speaker 7: I think it was clear to my family what I was going to be from an early age. I'm the eldest of five and my brothers and sisters always came to me for advice, and in the end, actually, my mother used to come to me for advice, or she'd talk things over, or as a family, we liked to try and find out why things happened as they did. I didn't really learn anything about it at school, but as part of biology, we did look at the way people behaved and why they do what they do. It was a long training, but something that's absolutely worthwhile. My belief in people, I suppose, is what made me choose this career. If there's anything I find disappointing, it's that if I've helped someone, I can't necessarily see the changes in their everyday lives.

Speaker 8: Yes, I was an only child, no brothers or sisters. My mother left my father when I was about seven so every holiday, I went to be with my father. I used to follow him everywhere and his job was a sports commentator. He travelled all over the place, following the races, and I went with him. It must have had a huge effect on me. I met all the famous drivers and the smell of the track, the noise from the cars and everything, was a very powerful thing that led me into this profession. Now I'm really doing it myself, I feel under pressure. I don't see enough of my own family, I'm travelling all over the world. So it's not the dream I thought it would be.

3   Check that the students know what the jobs are and ask them to discuss which are the most valuable to society.

4   Organise students so that they are now working with a different partner. Students compare the jobs they chose in the previous activity and explain their choices.

5   If necessary, explain that *perks* are features which may attract people to particular jobs. Ask students to brainstorm other advantages to add to the list (e.g. job security, regular hours, paid holidays, paid sick leave, gym membership, subsidised canteen).

6   Students prepare questions alone or in pairs (e.g. Are there any benefits to being self-employed? What are the drawbacks?). Write on the board all the different ideas that come from the students. Ask each person in the class to select one or two questions from the board.

Students should now mingle around the classroom, conducting a survey in which they interview as many students as they can and keep a note of the answers. If mingling is not possible, they can work together in large groups.

Students should give feedback to the rest of the class on the results of their survey. Wherever possible, they should comment on trends and tendencies rather than simply reporting the answers of individual students.

When discussing how to present the class findings, remind students of the desirability of having about five headings including an introduction and a conclusion. The information must be presented as clearly and unambiguously as possible. One of the easiest ways of ensuring clarity is to include paragraph or section headings.

Extension activity

Students write up their reports for homework.

To round-up, students should discuss which of the eight jobs appeals to them most. Encourage them to give reasons. Ask the class to feed back on their most interesting ideas.

Writing folder 3

Reports

1 Elicit from the class what a report is before doing the exercise. (A report is a formal written description of an event or situation. It may sometimes comment on positive and negative aspects and recommend possible improvements.)

Answers
a F They begin with a title and (usually) a statement of their purpose.
b T
c T This is not essential but it is a good idea to do this as you probably would when writing a report in 'real life'.
d F The aim of a report is more to inform than to interest.
e T
f F Both reports and proposals are likely to have these.
g F Reports do not always make recommendations but they often do.
h F They will usually be written in neutral or formal language.
i T
j F It is important for any task to spend time planning what you are going to write.

2 Before doing the exercise, remind students that Part 1 of the Writing Paper is a test of reading as well as writing.

Students should do the exercises individually before discussing as a whole class.

Extension activity

These are the key points that students should underline. Students may underline other points as well – this is unlikely to be a problem as long as they have underlined the phrases below.

You are studying at an international college in Ireland where you are on the student committee. The principal of the college has emailed you about underline{leisure facilities} offered by the college. Read the extract from the principal's email and some notes that you made at a meeting with other students. Then, using the information appropriately, write a underline{report} for the underline{principal} underline{commenting on the college's facilities} and underline{making recommendations for improvements}.
From: College Principal
To: Student Committee
Re: College Leisure Facilities
Could you, as a member of the student committee, please write a report on the leisure facilities which the college provides? I'm particularly keen to find out underline{attitudes to the sports centre and the music block}. I'd like to know whether students feel we provide appropriate facilities in these two areas and, if not, how they could be improved.

Notes from student meeting
underline{sports centre – great but heavily used (especially for tennis, swimming, basketball, fitness in gym)}
opening hours a bit short
need better booking system for gym
underline{music block – great practice rooms and instruments}
underline{any chance of larger hall} for performances, etc.?

3 Go through the questions quickly with the class as a whole.

Answers
a the principal of a college where you are studying
b neutral or formal
c information about leisure (sports and music) facilities at the college
d a report
e It is great but it is over-used (especially as far as some sports are concerned), the opening hours are too short and the gym could do with a better booking system.
f Practice rooms and instruments are great but students would like a larger hall there for concerts, etc.
g 180–220
h You should not lift language from the input text but should try to convey the ideas in different words.

4 Go through the Exam information box with students. Emphasise that these are precisely the questions that examiners ask themselves as they read any candidate's answer. Go through the questions, checking that students understand what they mean in practice. Students read the two responses and discuss them in pairs.

Suggested answers
Both answers are in accurate English. However, B would get an excellent mark while A would not. The problems with A are that:
• its language is too informal.
• it lifts too much from the input text.
• it is a letter and not a report.
• it is not organised into paragraphs.
• it introduces irrelevant material (e.g. about the library, which is not a leisure facility).
• it does not include all the necessary points (e.g. about the hall for the music block).

5 Ask students to write an answer to this task for homework. In a follow-up lesson, they should exchange answers with each other. Each student should check someone else's work using the questions listed in the Exam information box.

If appropriate, students can rewrite their work before submitting it to you for marking.

8 Being inventive

GENRE: Describing objects
TOPIC: Inventions

Speaking and reading	Twentieth-century inventions
Vocabulary	Positive and negative adjectives
Listening	What we can't live without
Grammar	Modals and semi-modals (2)
Speaking	Exclamations and fillers

Workbook contents

Use of English	Part 2 – open gap fill
Grammar	Modals and semi-modals (2)
Reading	Comprehension questions
Listening	Note completion

Student's book pages 52–55

Lesson planning
SV Vocabulary exercise 2 could be set for homework.
LV See extension activities in the Vocabulary and Grammar sections.

Speaking and Reading

1 Students should work with a partner to put the objects in the order in which they were invented.

Answers
1 wristwatch (1904)
2 electric dishwasher (1914)
3 sliced bread (1928)
4 the toaster (1937)
5 Biro pen (1948)
6 video recorder (1956)
7 ring-pull can (1962)
8 personal stereo (1979)
9 computer mouse (1984)
10 DVD player (1996)

2 Ask students to read about the inventions and then discuss the questions with a partner. You could ask students to give a score to each invention (1=terrible, 10=fantastic). As a class, compare the scores given for the different objects.

You may like to point out that all the inventions were patented (i.e. their inventors thought that they could become commercially successful).

Encourage a class discussion of the last question as a round up.

3 Students discuss their answers to the questions with a partner, using an English–English dictionary if necessary.

Answers
a
courting = the early stages of a romantic relationship
contours = shape
suction pad = piece of rubber that fixes itself to a smooth surface using suction
treadmill = wide wheel turned by people climbing on steps around its edge (used in the past to provide power for machines or as punishment)
mop = stick with material on one end for washing floors
pivotable = can be moved about a fixed point
b
mini- = small (e.g. *minimal, mini-series, miniskirt*)
c
-able = can or able to be (e.g. *disposable, regrettable, comparable*)
-less = without (e.g. *hopeless, thoughtless, careless*)
d
common ≠ separate
flexible ≠ inflexible, rigid
inner ≠ outer
drives ≠ halts, stops
mess up ≠ keep tidy
stowed ≠ unfolded

Vocabulary

1 Refer students to the Vocabulary spot and ask them to give other examples of adjectives conveying strong positive or negative feelings. Then ask students to work on this exercise with a partner, using a dictionary if necessary.

Answers

Positive	Negative
absorbing	grotesque
breathtaking	hackneyed
brilliant	hideous
delightful	ill-conceived
enchanting	impractical
engrossing	monstrous
ingenious	pointless
inspired	repulsive
ravishing	ridiculous
stunning	trivial

2 This could be set as homework to revise the work done in class.

Answers
a breathtaking
b ridiculous
c ingenious
d hackneyed
e stunning
f repulsive
g ill-conceived; delightful

3 Point out that students can write about the inventions on pages 52–53 or any other inventions that they choose.

Extension activity

Write the following adjectives on the board: *absorbing, breathtaking, delightful, enchanting, engrossing, grotesque, hackneyed, hideous, inspired, monstrous, ravishing, repulsive, ridiculous, stunning.* Ask students to suggest a noun that collocates with each of them.

Listening

1 Before looking at the photos, ask students to name some things that they could not live without.

1 12 Ask students to look at the pictures and listen to identify which things are mentioned by the speakers. Which other inventions or devices are mentioned?

Answers
Speaker 1: photo C, SatNav (air conditioning is also mentioned)
Speaker 2: photo D, the hair dryer (washing machines are also mentioned)
Speaker 3: photo A, contact lenses (microwaves are also mentioned)
Speaker 4: photo B, the mobile phone (the Internet is also mentioned)

2 **1 12**

Answers
a SatNav
b the washing machine
c microwave
d the internet

Recording script

Simon: OK, so the question is 'What couldn't you live without?' Is there anything that you just couldn't imagine life without?

Caroline: Yes, that's easy. Though it's something I used to think was a waste of money before I actually got one.

Ben: Don't tell me – it's your car. You spend most of your time driving.

Caroline: Nearly. It's my SatNav. We got it last year. It was just brilliant for getting from A to B. When we went on holiday last year, we programmed it to avoid the main roads and it took us on all sorts of back roads through the countryside. It's much better than stopping all the time, looking at the map, discovering you're lost and arguing. It took us to some stunning places we wouldn't have found otherwise. The air conditioning in the car is useful but I wouldn't say I couldn't live without that. Just open the window if it gets hot. What about you?

Annie: Well, because of the kids, the one thing I really couldn't do without is my washing machine, especially because we've got so much laundry to do. Nappies, as well, because we use washable nappies, which are more eco-friendly than the disposable ones.

Caroline: Oh yes. That's something most of us take for granted.

Annie: And ours is an inspired design, because it's got lots of features like the half-load button for example and er, it's ingenious the way it can do that. And the other thing I really couldn't do without is my hairdryer. Oh, I love my hairdryer! I think that's another piece of great design. Yeah, those are the things I really couldn't cope without.

Simon: I think I could easily do without mine.

Ben: That's only because you're getting a bit bald on top! I couldn't live without contact lenses. They're indispensable. Apart from being a brilliant invention, they – well, I couldn't see without them. I don't like wearing glasses – I'm quite vain – so I do need them. I mean, I think they're an absolutely extraordinary and inspired invention. But the other thing that I couldn't possibly live without is my microwave. The one I've got, it's a big hideous thing in the corner, is great because it can heat things up at the last minute. Cold cups of coffee suddenly become hot again, so I'm – er, without those two, with those two things I'm fine. Without them, I'd be lost. But what about you?

Simon: Me? Well, the first would have to be my mobile, of course. It's got lots of features – though I still mainly use it for phoning and texting and taking the odd photo if I don't have an actual camera to hand. It's just so convenient when you have to change arrangements at the last moment or when you want to keep in touch with people who aren't at home much. I wish its battery lasted longer – but apart from that, I've no complaints. My second thing would be the internet. Does that count?

Ben: As an invention? Why not?

Simon: OK, so that's what I'd go for then. It just makes it so easy to find information, to buy things – I get most of my books online and download most of my music, and movies. You can also make contact easily with people all over the world. I've done some great online courses, studying and meeting people who I'll probably never see face to face. I love it!

3   If necessary, play the recording again in order for students to hear the whole context in which each word was said.

> **Answers**
> **Positive:** brilliant, stunning, inspired, ingenious, indispensable, extraordinary
> **Negative:** vain, hideous

Modals and semi-modals (2)

1   The language here is covered on page 167 of the Grammar folder. Ask students to identify the modal verbs in the sentences.

> **Answers**
> a Someone really <u>ought to</u> invent a machine to do the ironing for you. (suggesting something would be a good idea)
> b This key ring bleeps when you whistle – that <u>should</u> help you next time you lose your keys. (suggesting something is likely)
> c You <u>must</u> get yourself a mobile phone – everyone else has got one. (giving advice)
> d My hairdryer's missing – my flatmate <u>must have</u> borrowed it again. (making a deduction)
> e You <u>should have</u> kept the instructions for the DVD recorder! (disapproval)
> f He submitted his request for a patent ages ago – he <u>must</u> be going to hear from the department soon. (probability)
> g You <u>shouldn't have</u> pressed that button before switching the power off. (he thinks the person did do something wrong)
> h The design has been approved and we <u>should</u> be starting production next week. (probability)
> i Even when he was still at school, he <u>would</u> spend hours in the shed designing weird and wonderful inventions. (frequently)
> j You <u>will</u> accept this design or else. (no choice)
> k We <u>must</u> light a fire somehow but no one's brought any matches – what <u>shall</u> we do? (suggestions)

2   Students should do this with a partner and then compare their answers with those of other students. It is not necessary to use any of the modals in the box more than once. As a follow-up, ask students the meaning of each modal used.

> **Answers**
> a must (obligation)
> b should / ought to (advice)
> c should have; must have (deduction)
> d would (past habit)
> e mustn't (prohibition)
> f should / ought to (advice)
> g Will (willingness)
> h shouldn't have (criticism)

ⓔxtension activity

Ask students what kind of invention they would like an inventor to design for them. They write some instructions, using modals. For example, *I'd like you to design a machine which will do the ironing for me. It must be able to recognise what type of material the clothes are made of and it should be able to adjust the temperature accordingly. It shouldn't cost more than £500 but it must be totally reliable …*
In a follow-up lesson, students could read out the descriptions of their inventions which they wrote in exercise 4 and the other students could award the inventions a mark out of ten as they did for the inventions in Reading exercise 1.

Corpus spot

> **Answers**
> a would   b should   c would   d would
> e should   f could

Speaking

1   Students often do not know quite what to say in English when they need to put in a supportive exclamation or word to show that they are listening attentively. Elicit the exclamations or attentive words that they have found useful and draw their attention to the Exam spot.

Before students do this, point out that different intonation can give these expressions quite differing meanings. They can all be made to sound ironic or bored, for example. In this exercise the aim is to go for the most usual use.

> **Answers**
> **expressing agreement:** a, i
> **expressing admiration:** b, g
> **expressing surprise or disbelief:** c, e, h, k, l, n
> **expressing sympathy:** d, f, j, m

2 Ask students to match the expressions in exercise 1 to
   sentences a–h.

> **Suggested answers**
> a Brilliant!   e Fantastic!
> b Poor you!   f Surely not!
> c You must be joking!   g Me too!
> d Oh dear!   h What a shame!

3 **1 13** Play the recording all the way through to allow
   students time to think about how they might respond.
   Then play the recording again, stopping after each
   snippet to allow students time to respond. Note that
   there are several different possible responses to each
   item.

> **Recording script (possible answers in brackets)**
> 1 The safety pin was invented in 1849. (No, really?)
> 2 I've got dreadful toothache! (Poor you!)
> 3 When Mrs Lincoln, the wife of President Lincoln,
>   had her photograph taken after her husband had
>   been assassinated, the photograph included a ghostly
>   image of the president. (How interesting!)
> 4 You have been selected to advise the Prime Minister
>   on the problems of education in this country.
>   (You're joking!)
> 5 My grandfather, my mother, my sister and I were
>   all born on the same date – the 6th of June! (What a
>   coincidence!)
> 6 There are 400 billion stars in the Milky Way. (That's
>   incredible!)
> 7 From 13th June 1948 to 1st June 1949, one person
>   in Los Angeles hiccupped 160 million times! 60,000
>   suggestions for cures were received before he
>   eventually stopped. (You must be joking!)
> 8 King Gustav II of Sweden thought that coffee was
>   poisonous. He once sentenced a man to death
>   by ordering him to drink coffee every day. The
>   condemned man in fact lived to be very old! (How
>   amazing!)
> 9 The first alarm clock was invented by Leonardo da
>   Vinci. It woke the sleeper by gently rubbing the soles
>   of his feet. (Fantastic!)
> 10 The common housefly carries 30 different diseases
>   which can be passed to humans. (No, really?)

4 Allow students a few moments to think of what they
   are going to tell their partner. As they talk, their partner
   is only allowed to use the exclamations worked on in
   this section.

Student's book pages 56–57

Paper 3 Part 4
Gapped sentences

1   Use the example to remind students of the format of the exercise. Ask them which of the three sentences the photo refers to. The answer is *notice*, which, like many words in English, has a number of different meanings in different contexts.

2   Do not spend too long on this activity. Its purpose is simply to make the point that there is unlikely to be a simple one-to-one translation for many English words.

Answers
bar = a place where drinks are served (noun); a long, rectangular shape, e.g. *a bar of chocolate* (noun); to prevent someone from doing something (verb)
flat = an apartment (noun); level and smooth (adjective); not interesting, or without emotion (adjective)
mean = to express an idea, thought or fact (verb); not kind (adjective); average (adjective)
put on = to gain weight (verb); to cover your body with clothes (verb); to produce (verb)
figures = numbers (noun); shapes (noun)

3   Students may prepare this exercise individ... home or in pairs in the classroom before che... through it in class.

Answers

1	mean	11	bar	21	bar
2	figures	12	flat	22	flat
3	Put on	13	figures	23	figures
4	flat	14	mean	24	bar
5	put on	15	flat	25	put on
6	bar	16	put on	26	flat
7	Mean	17	bar	27	figures
8	bar	18	figures	28	put on
9	flat	19	mean		
10	mean	20	put on		

4   If possible, students should use a good dictionary such as the *Cambridge Advanced Learner's Dictionary* to help them. When they read out their sentences to their partners they should 'blank' the word being focused on.

Going through the sentences in class should not take too long as the students' example sentences may well be quite similar.

Answers
set = to establish or cause to exist (verb); to put something in the stated position or place (verb); to get something ready so that it can be used (verb)
fair = right or reasonable (adjective); light-coloured, not dark (adjective); a large public event where goods are bought and sold (noun)
wind = a current of moving air (noun); to wrap around (verb); to turn something (verb)
stay = to remain in one place (verb); to live in a place (verb); a period of time that you spend in a place (noun)

5   Students sho... ...heir answers to this task at home bef... ...m in class.

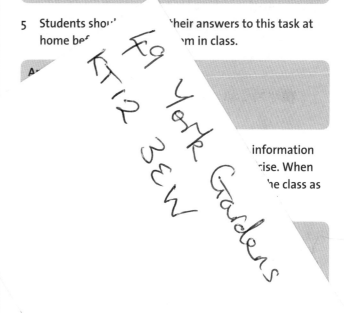

...information ...ise. When ...he class as

9 I have a dream

GENRE: Speeches
TOPIC: Social change

Reading	Martin Luther King's *I have a dream* speech
Listening	Martin Luther King's speech (continued) and other speeches
Vocabulary	Metaphors and idioms
Grammar	Future forms
Speaking	Social change
Workbook contents	
Listening	Multiple-choice questions
Grammar	Future forms
Vocabulary	Metaphor and idiom
Use of English	Part 2 – open gap fill

Student's book pages 58–61

Lesson planning

SV Vocabulary exercises 1 or 2 and Grammar exercises 1 or 2 could be set for homework.

LV See extension activities in the Reading, Listening and Grammar sections.

Reading

1 You might like to point out that the speech that students will read and listen to in this lesson has been labelled a C2-level text, because of its rich and complex language, and also because it demonstrates a very sophisticated use of language intended to inspire and affect its audience. Discuss the warm-up questions with the class as a whole. Allow for students to interpret *speeches* as widely as they wish (i.e. any extended piece of speaking to an audience). It could be a speech at a wedding or other family function, for example, or on an academic topic to classmates.

Background information
The person in the photo is Martin Luther King, an African American clergyman and civil rights campaigner. He delivered the *I have a dream* speech on the steps at the Lincoln Memorial in Washington DC on August 28, 1963, as the climax of a civil rights march on Washington. He was advocating a non-violent approach to his campaigners but was himself assassinated five years later.

2 Students read the speech extract then choose the sentences which best sum up each paragraph.

Answers
1 d 2 a 3 e 4 b

Go over any major language difficulties that students may be having with the speech but try to get them to feel the mood of the speech rather than to worry too much about details.

3 Discuss this question with the class as a whole.

Extension activity

Ask the following extra questions for the reading text.
- What is King's purpose in this part of the speech?
- What do you think the dream that he has will be?
- What do you think he might say in the rest of the speech?

Answers
His purpose in this part of the speech was to rouse his listeners to press for action by pointing out that one hundred years after the freeing of slaves in the US, black people still did not enjoy freedom.

The last two questions are simply conjecture at this point. Encourage students to give their ideas but do not comment on how accurately they have guessed.

Listening

1 🔊 **14** Before students listen to the next part of the speech, make sure that they understand all the points they are to listen out for. Go through the list with them and elicit an example of each of the points listed. Then play the rest of the speech, while the students listen and tick the relevant items on the list.

Answers
Techniques that you should tick are listed below with some examples in brackets (other examples may also be found for many of these points).
- repetition (*Go back to, I have a dream ...*)
- mixing short and long sentences (mainly long sentences followed by the final short one)
- addressing the audience directly (*I say to you today, my friends, ...*)
- making use of metaphor (*sweltering with the heat of injustice, an oasis of freedom and justice*)
- quoting famous lines (*We hold these truths to be self-evident: that all men are created equal* – from the American Declaration of Independence)
- making dramatic pauses
- appealing to the audience's emotions (almost all the speech)

Recording script

Go back to Mississippi, go back to Alabama, go back to South Carolina, go back to Georgia, go back to Louisiana, go back to the slums and ghettos of our northern cities, knowing that somehow this situation can and will be changed. Let us not wallow in the valley of despair.

I say to you today, my friends, so even though we face the difficulties of today and tomorrow, I still have a dream. It is a dream deeply rooted in the American dream.

I have a dream that one day this nation will rise up and live out the true meaning of its creed: 'We hold these truths to be self-evident: that all men are created equal.'

I have a dream that one day on the red hills of Georgia the sons of former slaves and the sons of former slave owners will be able to sit down together at the table of brotherhood.

I have a dream that one day even the state of Mississippi, a state sweltering with the heat of injustice, sweltering with the heat of oppression, will be transformed into an oasis of freedom and justice.

I have a dream that my four little children will one day live in a nation where they will not be judged by the color of their skin but by the content of their character. I have a dream today.

Extension activity

Ask students to look again at the first part of the speech and see if any of the techniques that were not ticked in Listening exercise 1 are exemplified.

Answers
alliteration (*dark and desolate*)

2   Students identify the types of speech in each photo.

Answers
A   a Best Man's speech
B   a school assembly
C   a slideshow presentation
D   a farewell speech

3   🔊 15 Students listen and try to identify the occasions.

Answers
1   a wedding reception
2   a talk in a school assembly
3   a presentation
4   a colleague's last day at work

4   Give each student one or two of the techniques from the list in Listening exercise 1 to listen out for. They should note down the examples of the techniques which they hear. After listening, go through the

speeches one by one and ask students to report back on any examples of points that they found. Students may come up with other suggestions that you find acceptable but some of the main techniques used in these speeches are indicated here in brackets after the relevant places in the script.

Recording script

Speaker 1: We've known each other since our first day at school when we were five (*presenting interesting or surprising facts*). We were two scared little boys sitting at the same table hoping that we were going to enjoy this strangely exciting new world (*appealing to the audience's emotions*). Now he is beginning another new stage of his life. In some ways it may be rather like starting school again (*making analogies or comparisons*). Especially, of course, as his beautiful bride (*appealing to the audience's senses*) is a teacher herself. So now he's the teacher's favourite – something none of the staff at our old school would ever have expected! (*humour*)

Speaker 2: You may not believe it of an old man like me, but it seems no time at all (*exaggeration*) to me since I had a 'shining morning face', as Shakespeare so aptly put it (*quoting famous lines*), a face that was once as young and eager as the ones I see before me now. I too was dreaming of a life beyond the confines of these walls (*making analogies or comparisons*). I promised your headmaster that I would neither be too sentimental or too long-winded. I suppose I'd better change track before I fail on the sentimental count, but I promise to do my best to be brief. (*humour, appealing to the audience's senses*)

Speaker 3: This next slide (*using visual aids*) shows the narrow pathway down to Petra, the 'rose-red city half as old as time' (*quoting famous lines*). It might be one of the hottest days of your whole trip (*appealing to the audience's senses*) but who could not be impressed by the glorious red-sandstone buildings of this city, reputedly the oldest city in the world? (*asking rhetorical questions*) Once known as Palmyra, it grew in importance because of its location, enabling it to control the trade routes of the ancient world (*presenting interesting or surprising facts*).

Speaker 4: Well, Fiona. You've been working here (*drawing attention to the location where the speech is taking place*) for longer than any of us, including the boss, and we're all going to miss you very much. We've clubbed together to get you this little token of our appreciation for all the good – and occasionally not so good – times we've shared together (*appealing to the audience's emotions*). We hope that whenever you make yourself some coffee you'll think of us and the thousands of coffees we've shared over the years. Remember us all whenever you drink a cappuccino. All the very best for a long, happy and healthy retirement.

Vocabulary

A metaphor is an expression that describes a person, object or something else in a literary way by referring to something that is considered to possess similar characteristics to the person or object that is being described, e.g. *Her words cut into him.* (Here, her obviously sharp or unkind words are compared to a knife, in that they hurt him.)

An idiom is a group of words in a fixed order having a different meaning from each word understood on its own, e.g. *to give someone a hand* (to help someone).

Many idioms are also metaphors – but metaphors can only also be called idioms if they have a fixed format and are in common use.

1 Work through the exercise as a class. As you deal with each item, ask students to explain what the relevance of the metaphor is in each case. Draw students' attention to the Vocabulary spot at this point.

> **Answers**
> a punishment
> b light, punishment
> c light
> d heat
> e economics
> f nature, light
> g nature, heat
> h nature

2 Ask students to look at the idioms in italics and check the meanings of any that they do not understand. They should then try to complete the exercise. Remind them that they will sometimes need to change the form of the idiom slightly so that it fits the grammar of the sentence. As you check the answers, ask students to explain what each idiom means in non-idiomatic English.

> **Answers**
> a *foot the bill* (= will pay)
> b *went up in smoke* (= vanished)
> c *am tied up* (= am busy)
> d *feel all at sea* (= not knowing what you should do)
> e *shedding light on* (= clarifying)
> f *light dawned* (= she realised)
> g *common ground* (= points that could be agreed on)
> h *put its money where its mouth is* (= be prepared to spend money as well as to talk)
> i *will get your fingers burnt* (= will get into trouble)

3 Ask students to work alone to create their sentences. Then, they work with a partner to compare what they wrote. Encourage students to ask each other questions to find out more information.

Future forms

The language here is covered on page 167 of the Grammar folder.

1 Before looking at the section with students, brainstorm as many ways of talking about the future as possible and elicit the point that the choice of form made will depend on the meaning the user wants to convey (e.g. degree of certainty in the user's mind) and grammatical constraints.

Students then discuss the exercise with a partner before checking their answers. Deal with any issues that arise as difficulties for the class as a whole.

> **Answers**
> a 5   b 1   c 6   d 4,6   e 8   f 9   g 7   h 3
> i 10   j 2

2 Work through this exercise with the whole class.

> **Answers**
> a I'm going
> b get
> c we'll be lying
> d he'd leave
> e to get
> f leaves / is leaving
> g are, are going to spend
> h gets, she's going to study
> i will have set foot

3 Students practise the questions in pairs. Monitor as they do so, to check that they are using the correct forms.

> **E**xtension activity
>
> Do some quick class practice of the questions in Future forms exercise 1, choosing students at random to answer each of the questions and some variations on them. For example, ask:
> • *What are you doing this weekend?*
> • *What will you be doing this time next week?*

4 Elicit what the situation is in the photo. Ask students to write sentences about what might happen using as many different future forms (in appropriate ways) as they can. When they are ready, students take turns to read out their sentences to the class.

Speaking

1 Briefly discuss some of the issues in the list with the class before starting this activity. Pick on aspects of these topics that the class are most likely to feel strongly about and to feel that there is a need for change. Point out that they do not have to choose one of the issues from the page – anything that concerns them will be appropriate as long as they all agree that changes are necessary. Encourage them to think of at least three or four specific changes that they would like to make with regard to their chosen subject.

2 Allow plenty of time for students to discuss their chosen issue.

3 Encourage students to think about how to give the report. After each presentation is given, invite a student to present the notes he or she made while listening. The group who made the presentation should then comment on how accurate those notes were.

In their original groups, students discuss the presentations they heard. They can decide which was the most effective, and which changes seemed most acceptable.

Writing folder 4

Student's book pages 62–63

Describing a novel

This Exam folder helps students prepare for the optional question in the Writing test (Paper 2), which asks candidates to write about a text they have read beforehand (the set text).

As it is impossible to provide work for specific set texts, this Writing folder looks at general aspects of working with set texts for the exam. Make sure your students are clear that they are not expected to write answers with an academic literary focus. It is not a literature test. Candidates are encouraged to read for pleasure and because it will improve their knowledge of English, not because they are expected to develop literary appreciation skills.

1 and 2 Encourage students to think of two books they know well and can talk about. These should be fiction books. If you know students are reading a set text in preparation for the exam, encourage them to talk about this. If you do not know what the set texts are

for the current exam, you will be able to find out from the Cambridge ESOL website.

The answers below give some common topics for a question on a set text. However, there are many other equally valid topics that the students may come up with.

Possible answers
most interesting character; key moment in the plot; relationship between two main characters and how this develops during the story; the way the writer interests the reader in reading more; the importance of the place where the story is set; the importance of the period when the story is set; the significance of the title of the story; whether the story makes / would make a good film; whether the story resonates with anything in the students' own lives; anything unsuccessful about the story; how appropriate the story is for someone learning English

3 This activity may be done in pairs or small groups. Allow plenty of time for discussion as this may encourage students to read the books they hear about. It would also be possible to follow up by asking students to write a review of their book.

4 Ask students to plan their answer carefully and to prepare the first draft of the review. Students should write approximately 240 words. Draw their attention to the topics in exercise 3.

When students exchange their first drafts, encourage constructive criticism and a keen eye for errors.

5 The answers below give some characteristics of articles, reports, reviews and essays, which students should be aware of.

Possible answers
Article: written for a large audience, about whom the writer knows little beyond the fact that they read a magazine of a particular type; benefits from a title and an opening sentence that will intrigue readers and encourage them to read on; aim is to interest
Report: mainly concerned with facts; has to be clearly organised and expressed; headings may be a useful way of guiding both the reader and writer through the text; it is often necessary to finish with a recommendation and if so the reasons for the recommendation should be clearly and unambiguously stated; aim is to inform
Review: the reader wants to get a general impression of what is being reviewed but does not want a detailed description of the plot; aim is to help the reader decide whether to read the book or watch the film for themselves
Essay: written for a teacher and so is likely to be in a neutral to formal style; should be clearly structured and logically argued; aim is to impress in terms of both content and style

10 You live and learn

GENRE: Academic texts
TOPIC: Further study

Reading	Academic texts
Vocabulary	Word formation
Grammar	Participle clauses
Speaking	Contrastive stress
Workbook contents	
Reading	Multiple-choice questions
Listening	Multiple-choice questions
Vocabulary	Matching meanings to definitions; word formation
Grammar	Participle clauses
Writing	A report

Student's book pages 64–67

Lesson planning
SV   Vocabulary exercises 1 or 2 could be set for homework.
LV   See extension activities in the Reading, Vocabulary and Speaking sections.

Reading

1   The aim of these questions is to raise interest in the topic of studying in English, something which students may be increasingly likely to do in the future. Students discuss the questions in pairs. Encourage them to support their answers with reasons and examples. Round up ideas with the whole class.

2   These texts have been labelled as being at C2 level. Not only is the vocabulary very sophisticated, but the subject matter is highly specialised and likely to sometimes be outside students' field of interest. Encourage students to read the texts as quickly as possible to get an idea of what they are about, and to match them with the subjects.

Answers
1 sociolinguistics   4 economics
2 history   5 law
3 psychology

Students then match the texts with the pictures.

Answers
1 E   2 B   3 D   4 A   5 C

Now allow time for students to read the texts more fully in order to be able to answer question c. They should decide on a title with a partner and then compare their answers with those suggested by other students.

Suggested answers
1 The observation of language change
2 Changes in 18th-century Russian life
3 Consumerism prevails
4 Minority in law
5 Experiments in extra-sensory perception

3   Point out that academic language – whatever the subject – often uses language that is rather different from everyday spoken language. However, text 3 is written in a far less formal style than the others, while text 4 is the most formal and academic in tone. Encourage students to look at the words and phrases in their context and try to work out the meaning before choosing their answers from the options in the box.

Answers
a resounding negative – a firm no
as a prelude to – before
hitherto – previously
in arrears – behind
spending power – spare money
saturation – stage where nothing more is needed
attains – reaches
formerly – previously
leave – permission
obtain – get
vice versa – the other way round
differentiate – make a difference between

4   Set this for homework if time is short and check the answers in a follow-up lesson.

Answers
a saturation   e in arrears
b differentiate   f obtain
c vice versa   g formerly
d leave   h spending power

Vocabulary

1   Students do as much as they can first and then use a dictionary to complete the table, if necessary.

Suggested answers

Verb	Noun	Adjective
occur	occurrence	occurring
found	founder	founding
–	consequence	consequent, consequential
oblige	obligation	obligatory
disappear	disappearance	disappearing
glamorise	glamour	glamorous
authorise	authority	authoritative, authorised
vary	variety	various
presume	presumption	presumptuous
perceive	perception	perceptive, perceptible

2   Ask students to try this exercise individually before discussing it with the class as a whole.

Suggested answers

a   It is **obligatory** for (all) pupils to wear school uniform.
b   There is a wide/large/great **variety** of animals which are indigenous to Australia.
c   Burglaries are an everyday **occurrence** in this part of town.

d   The mountaineer is **presumed** to have died in the blizzard.
e   Giving up work to bring up a child and the **consequent** loss of income are difficult for many women.
f   How do people in your country **perceive** the role of the United Nations? / How is the role of the United Nations perceived in your country?
g   Cambridge University Press was **founded** in 1534.
h   Modern films tend to **glamorise** violence.

Participle clauses

Discuss the examples and the introduction with the class as a whole. The language here is covered on page 168 of the Grammar folder.

1   Do the first question in the exercise with the class as a whole. Then ask students to complete the exercise in pairs before comparing answers with the whole class.

Possible answers

a   Because he hoped to gain a speedy victory, the general took the decision to invade.
b   Since it was a Sunday, most of the shops were shut.
c   Charles I, who was generally considered a weak king, was eventually beheaded.
d   As Picton had previously learned their language, he was able to communicate with the tribe.
e   When you have measured the wood carefully, cut as indicated.
f   Although Charlton's work was ignored until recently by many scholars, it is at last getting the recognition it deserves.
g   If it is seen from a distance, the castle looks like something out of a fairy tale.

2 Go through the Corpus spot before exercise 2. Ask students to complete this exercise individually. Then check the answers with the class as a whole, discussing any problems that arise. While doing this exercise, draw attention to the three basic types of participle phrase: those beginning with an *-ing* word; those with a past participle; and those with *having* + a past participle.

Suggested answers
a Walking round the exhibition, I caught sight of an old school friend at the far end of the gallery.
b Having made so many mistakes in her homework, Marti had to do it all over again.
c Being only a child, she can't understand what is happening.
d Not knowing anyone in the town to spend the evening with, Jack decided to have an early night.
e Looked at from a sociological point of view, the problem can be seen as one of tension between social classes.

3 Students work with a partner to complete the sentences in any way that they wish. Write two or three of the best answers for each on the board.

Possible answers
a Having studied English for some years now, I feel quite confident about using the language.
b Having spent a lot of time trying to master the piano, I've accepted that I'll never be a great player.
c It being a sunny day today, I think we should go to the beach.
d Not wanting to appear boastful, I must tell you that my English pronunciation has often been praised.
e Knowing what I know now about Mary, I wish I'd trusted her more.

🅣eaching extra

Although students may well have few difficulties understanding this structure, they are likely to be rather slow at using it in their own written work. When you mark any free writing from your students over the next few weeks, try to suggest ways in which they could have used it in their work. This may encourage them to use it themselves in future writing.

Speaking

1 Ask students to discuss which words Speaker B would be likely to stress.

2 🔊1 16 Play the recording for students to check their answers. The words which are stressed are underlined in the script.

Recording script
1 A: Did you go to the cinema last night?
  B: No, but I went to the <u>theatre</u>.
2 A: Did you go by bike to the theatre last night?
  B: No, <u>Marco</u> was using my bike last night.
3 A: Did you go to the theatre by bus last night?
  B: No, I went to the theatre by <u>taxi</u> last night.
4 A: Did you go home by taxi last night?
  B: No, I went home by taxi <u>two</u> nights ago.
5 A: Anna's wearing a lovely green dress.
  B: It's a green <u>blouse</u> and <u>skirt</u>, actually.
6 A: Did you have a good time at the party last night?
  B: Yes, we had a <u>brilliant</u> time.
7 A: Are you hungry yet?
  B: I'm not <u>hungry</u>, I'm <u>starving</u>.
8 A: Are you hungry yet?
  B: <u>I'm</u> not hungry but <u>Tina</u> is.

3 Ask students to work with a partner. Have some initial prompts ready to suggest to students who may find this difficult (e.g. *Does Mary love Bobby? Did you have tomato soup for lunch today?*)

4 Students should practise reading the conversations, with each student having the opportunity to be both A and B.

🅔xtension activity

Students pass their conversations to another pair of students who read them out, stressing the important words to the rest of the class. The other students should note down which words they think are being stressed.

5 Refer students to the Exam spot at this point. Practise one or two sentences describing the differences between the pictures with the class as a whole. Then ask students to work with a partner and to take care to stress the important words in an appropriate way. Encourage students to use contrastive word stress where appropriate.

Units 6–10 Revision

Students' book pages 68–69

Topic review

Ask students to work with a partner to discuss questions a–j. The aim of this exercise is to encourage students to recycle the vocabulary and structures they have covered in the preceding units in a personalised way.

Grammar

1 Students could prepare their answers to the questions for homework. Encourage students to write two or three full sentences in answer to each of the questions. Students should work with a partner, taking turns to ask each other questions a–f.

2 and 3 Students work alone before comparing answers in pairs.

Reading

1 Check that students know what *telecommuting* is (= working from home rather than going to work in an office and instead communicating with one's office by phone, email, etc.).

2 When checking the answers together, encourage students to explain how they knew what the right answer was in each case.

Answers
C, E, F, B, D, A, G

Vocabulary

1 Students do this individually and then compare their answers with a partner.

Answers
a fair
b draw
c hit
d bear
e bar

2 Refer students to the Exam spot. Before doing the exercise, look at the words in the box and discuss what other words could be formed from the same roots. Students then do the exercise and compare their answers.

Answers
1 out   5 out
2 to   6 all
3 of   7 in
4 According 8 brand

GENRE: Articles
TOPIC: Fashion

Reading	Talking clothes
Listening	Dress codes
Grammar	Reported speech
Speaking	Comparing
Workbook contents	
Reading	Putting missing sentences into gaps
Vocabulary	Gap-fill from reading exercise
Grammar	Reported speech
Use of English	Part 3 – word formation

Student's book pages 70–73

Lesson planning	
SV	Reading exercise 4 could be set for homework.
LV	See the extension activity in the Listening section.

Reading

1 Introduce the unit by asking students to discuss questions a–e with a partner.

  a Depending on the age and interests of your students, you can use this question to discuss a range of things: clothes, electronic gadgets, music, etc.

  b This question focuses students on the topic of clothes.

  c This question could lead to a short discussion of the influence of advertising.

  d This question might stimulate debate on whether people read more than before because we use the Internet more, or less because they prefer watching TV or looking at images online. Students might compare the feel of real paper in their hands as opposed to reading from a screen. You could also discuss whether reading a magazine or a newspaper in certain situations (e.g. at a café, on a train, at the breakfast table) can be replaced by reading from an electronic device.

  e Discuss the headlines with the class. If possible, have some more examples of English-language magazines to bring to class or if you have access to the Internet, look up some magazine sites, and find more headlines to discuss.

2 You could develop the discussion by asking if there is a difference between men's and women's attitudes to shopping and whether it is better to go shopping for clothes on your own or with a friend.

Ask students to read the base text first. Then they should read paragraphs A–G and fit them into gaps 1–6. Remind students to look for reasons for their choices based on meaning and grammar.

Answers
1 C 2 Γ 3 A 4 G 5 D 6 E

3 Go through the article and paragraphs, helping students to find reasons for their answers.

4 This exercise could be set for homework. Point out to students that they should always try to notice new or interesting vocabulary when they read in English, paying special attention to collocations and fixed phrases.

Answers
a	a good fit	e	tailoring
b	a garment	f	racks (of clothing)
c	bespoke	g	suit (it suits you)
d	a tape measure	h	strip off

Listening

1 Refer students to the Exam spot. Then use exercise 1 to introduce the topic of dress codes.

Extension activity

Ask students what they would expect the following people to wear (male and female versions): a lawyer, a doctor, an architect, a teacher, a shop assistant in a clothes shop, a bus driver, a flight attendant.

2 This prediction exercise will prepare students for the listening. If your students need help, lead the discussion with the following questions.

- *In which jobs is appearance important?*
- *What do you think 'dress-down Friday' is?*
- *What is body jewellery?*
- *Why might some people object to a dress code?*

3 **1 17** Explain that students will hear the exact words they need to fill the gaps on the recording.

Answers

a	reception	f	(a) training day(s)
b	a tie and a dark suit	g	a nose ring
c	accountants	h	civil liberties
d	dress-down Friday	i	Human Resources
e	smart-casual		

Recording script

Now, it's been brought to my attention that certain members of staff have been flouting the dress code. So I want to make it crystal clear to everyone just exactly what's expected. Those of you who work at the reception must be – how shall I put it – business-like at all times. That's the look we want to achieve. You are the first people that visitors see when they enter the building. Whether they then go on to the managing director or the canteen is irrelevant. You create the first impression of the company, and as we all know, first and last impressions count. Now, for men that means wearing a tie and a dark suit. For women, a suit, that can be a tailored trouser suit, or a smart dress or skirt and jacket. Blouses must be short- or long-sleeved, not sleeveless. It goes without saying that hair and so on needs to be neat and tidy.

Now, as for accountants … You never know when a client may come in to see you. You may think you're not in the public relations business but in a way, you are. And I know most of the time people make appointments, but there are occasions when someone just happens to be in the area and decides to drop in. In this case, you represent us. This is a firm with a good reputation. Clients expect their accountant to reflect this, not only in their work but also in the way they present themselves. Don't forget, in many people's eyes, sloppy clothes means sloppy work, and I must say, I tend to agree.

The only possible exception to this is dress-down Friday. But this only applies if you have no appointments with clients in your diary. Now, this doesn't mean that you can turn up wearing whatever you like – no shorts and sandals, please! It's got to be 'smart-casual'. That's what it says here. But you can wear smart jeans and a jacket or even a sweater.

Now, something's come to my attention that I'm not at all happy about – training days. It seems as though some of you have got the idea into your head that when you're on a training day, that means you can dress like a student. It does not. You're still a representative of this company. When you go out to the business college, you're judged there too. I've heard remarks about one person who turned up there wearing a nose ring. This is not acceptable; it's all in the company's dress code, which you've all had a copy of. What I want to emphasise is that it's a matter of professional pride, the way you dress.

I know some people start complaining about civil liberties and all that, but I'm sorry, as I see it, we're all here to do a job. We are employees of a company, and we have to toe the line, and not only in what we do and how we do our job, but also in the way we dress.

If anyone feels particularly aggrieved by any of this, all I can say is that you take it up with the Human Resources department. Go up to the fifth floor, you know, next to the UK Sales department.

But really, I hope I won't have to refer to this again and I expect to see a dramatic improvement in personal presentation.

4 Ask this question to round off the topic.

Reported speech

The language here is covered on page 168 of the Grammar folder.

1 Ask students to work with a partner, then talk through the 'rules' as necessary. The aim here is to consolidate and extend students' range of reporting verbs and to point out that we do not always change the verb tense.

Suggested answers

a exactly what was/is expected.
b those of us who work/worked on reception must/had to be businesslike at all times.
c us that in many people's eyes, sloppy clothes meant/means sloppy work.
d she was/is not at all happy about the way some people dressed/dress for training days.
e it seemed/seems as though some of us had/have got the idea into our head that when we were/are on a training day we could/can dress like a student.
f had turned up wearing a nose ring.
g it was/is a matter of professional pride, the way we dress/dressed.
h we had/have to toe the line.
i if anyone felt/feels particularly aggrieved by any of that/this, all she could say was/is that we should take it up with the Human Resources department.
j she wouldn't / won't have to refer to this/that again.

2 The structures which follow certain reporting verbs can be problematic for students. The aim of this activity is to raise students' awareness of various structures and to provide practice of them.

Answers
doing it: b, g, h, i, n
to do it: a, c, e, f, m
me (not) to do it: d, e, g, j, k
that (I) should do it: b, c, h, l

3 This gives students practice of reported questions. Ask them to read through the questions on their own and to add two more. Students interview each other and note down the replies they get to questions. They then write a summary of the interview using reported speech. The summary could be set for homework.

Corpus spot

Go through the information in the Corpus spot with students. Ask students to focus on the the reporting verbs in each sentence and the structures which follow.

Answers
1 It is **recommended** to book in advance.
2 I would recommend **asking / that you ask** for further information.
3 **We were told that** the problems **would be solved / were going to be solved**.
4 It has been suggested **that we have** a film club once a month.
5 He suggested **asking Colin / that you ask Colin** to make the opening speech.
6 She regrets **not having** enough time to play an instrument.
7 We promised **(that) there** would be 35 stalls at the charity day.
8 I **recommend / would suggest** that you leave the train at the station of Morges.

Speaking

1 Go through the information in the Exam spot which is about Part 2 of the Speaking test (Paper 5). Explain that when students compare two or more things, they can talk about the similarities and differences between them. Using appropriate connecting devices will help students structure their speaking.

Answers
Talking about similarities
is similar to the other (picture) in that …
shows the same kind of …
like the second (picture), …
is much the same as …

Talking about differences
However,
although
on the one hand,
on the other hand,
while

2 Ask students to look at photos A and B while they discuss which plan or part of a plan they think they will use. All these plans are good. It may depend on the photos and the task as to which plan is most suitable. You could ask students which plan they think they would use in the exam.

3 **1 18** Ask students to answer the questions as they listen to the recording.

Answers
a plan 3
b *but, and, in contrast* (and students' own answers)
c flamboyant
d a teacher

Recording script
Examiner: In this part of the test, I'm going to give each of you some pictures. I'd like you to talk about them on your own for about a minute, and also to answer a question briefly about your partner's pictures. Angela, it's your turn first. Here are your pictures A and B. They show people wearing different types of clothes. I'd like you to compare the pictures and say why these people may have chosen to wear these clothes and what the clothes might tell us about the wearer. All right?

Angela: OK, in photos A and B, they are both pictures of men but they are wearing very different clothes. In picture A, we can see a man wearing a suit and in fact the stripes are quite prominent; it's not a subtle sort of stripe that the typical businessman wears. And there's another interesting thing about the suit; it's shiny – that's quite flamboyant. Then this man is wearing a tie – sort of pink with deeper stripes. Again, that's outrageous, some might say.

This leads me to think that perhaps he's not a businessman who works in a bank or insurance company but perhaps he's something to do with the arts or in advertising. It's got to be a profession which allows him to express his slightly extrovert personality.

In contrast, in photo B, there's a man wearing casual clothes. He's wearing some sort of brown top with a zip and then over that he's got another blue jacket which is undone. It looks as if it's made of that fleece material. He's got a scarf tucked into his top. His trousers have got large pockets on the sides of the legs – quite fashionable, I think. I'm not absolutely sure but perhaps they might be made of corduroy. And then he's wearing walking boots.

Looking at this picture, I would say this man is enjoying some time at the weekend, out in the country – he's a man who loves being out in nature and he's quite a free thinker. I can't imagine him working in a bank either – look at his hair. He could be a teacher.

Examiner: Thank you. Now, Luciano, which picture shows the clothes that you would be most comfortable wearing?

Luciano: Oh, definitely picture B. I feel much better when I'm wearing casual clothes and I would certainly never wear a suit like that!

Examiner: Thank you.

ⓣeaching extra

In the exam, there is often a tendency for the candidate who comments on the other candidate's long turn to talk for too long. However, the comment should be brief – only about 30 seconds are allowed.

4   Go through the notes and then brainstorm other phrases Angela could have used in her talk.

Suggested answers

I'd like to choose pictures A and B. Although they are both pictures of men, they show very different types of people, I think mainly because of the clothes they are wearing and the setting.

Pictures A and B look interesting because, although they are both pictures of men, the different characters come across in the clothes they are wearing.

5   Divide students into groups of three. One student is the Examiner, one is Student A and one is Student B. Give A and B five minutes to prepare for their long turn. They should plan an opening line, consider some of the similarities/differences they want to talk about and think about linking devices to use. During this time, the Examiner should also think about the questions. The group should then go through the whole speaking task. At the end, the Examiner comments on how effective A and B's answers were.

Exam folder 5

Student's book pages 74–75

Paper 3 Part 5
Key word transformations

Read through the introduction to Part 5 of the Use of English test and draw attention to the example.

1

Answers
a The essay <u>made an impression on</u> me.
b Sarah <u>insisted on (only) speaking</u> English with the visitors.
c There was a <u>sharp increase in</u> the price of petrol last month.
d I <u>caught sight of</u> the postman for a minute as he passed by my window.

2 Ask students to work with a partner to discuss the mistakes.

Answers
a The phrasal verb is *to hand something down to someone* – *to* is missing.
   The secret recipe <u>is handed down to</u> each new generation.
b The given word is in the past tense and cannot be changed.
   The present <u>came as a complete surprise</u> to me.
c The spelling of *emotion* is wrong.
   The child's mother <u>was overcome with emotion</u> when he was found.
d The idiom for *to help someone* is *to give someone a hand*.
   Could you possibly <u>give me a hand</u> with this suitcase?

3 Go through the introduction to fixed phrases and collocations. Ask students to work with a partner.

Answers
1 b   2 e   3 a   4 f   5 c   6 d

4 As examples, elicit the prepositions that are needed after *make an impression* (*on*), *insist* (*on*), *to be overcome* (*with*).

Answers
a in   c from   e with
b of   d in   f in

5 Elicit examples of sentences containing the passive form, conditional forms and reported speech.

Answers
a If we don't get the 8 o'clock train, <u>it will mean missing</u> lunch.
b Italian football players are <u>said to get the highest</u> salaries.
c The tour operator <u>apologised for not</u> emailing the details earlier.
d Your accountant <u>should have given you</u> better advice.

6 This exam practice could be set as homework.

Answers
a A medical certificate <u>wasn't required for</u> my US visa.
b The island <u>is rich in</u> natural resources.
c Gina <u>does nothing but</u> complain.
d The candidate <u>gave honest answers to</u> the questions.
e If the tennis court <u>hadn't been so wet</u>, the match wouldn't have been cancelled.
f I'd <u>be on your side</u> even if you weren't my friend.
g He <u>flatly refused to</u> help me.
h Could you get some fruit <u>on your way</u> home?

12 Leaf through a leaflet

GENRE: Information pages
TOPIC: Making decisions

Speaking	Types of information pages
Reading and writing	Leaflet on career opportunities
Listening	Designing a leaflet
Grammar	*-ing* forms
Speaking	Making decisions
Workbook contents	
Grammar	*-ing* forms
Listening	Matching options to speakers
Vocabulary	Tourism
Reading	Understanding a leaflet

Student's book pages 76–79

Lesson planning
SV Grammar exercise 2 could be set for homework.
LV See the extension activity in the Listening section.

Speaking

1   Refer to the title of the unit and elicit the meaning of *to leaf through*. You leaf through a book or a magazine by turning the pages quickly and reading only a little of it (e.g. *I was leafing through magazines in the airport shop.*). Make sure students notice the word *leaf* in *leaflet*.

   a   Ask students to work in pairs and discuss the questions.

Answers
A a brochure   C a leaflet
B a prospectus   D a flier

   b   A leaflet is a piece of paper, or sometimes several pieces of paper folded or fixed together like a book, which gives you information or advertises something (e.g. *They were handing out leaflets on the street.*).

   c   It could be said that leaflets are an effective means of communication because they are usually compact, clearly written, have a good layout and give essential information.

   d   Elicit the phrase *an informed decision*. Generally speaking, good decisions are based on appropriate information.

2   Ask students to change partners to discuss the questions. When students have finished, ask them to summarise their opinions for the whole class.

Reading and Writing

1   Ask students to scan the leaflet quickly to find the answers to the questions.

Suggested answers
a   It gives examples of jobs that modern languages students go into and gives information on what employers look for.
b   to encourage/help students think about their career options
c   Headings and bullet points make it easier to find information. Short sentences/phrases and single words make it quick to read and easy to understand.
d   neutral, informative, impersonal

2   Make sure students plan their leaflets: choose the three points, write headings and then discuss what to include in each paragraph.

Listening

Refer students to the Exam spot. Explain that in Part 2 of the Listening test (Paper 4), students are required to listen to a text for specific information. Reading the questions before listening is essential so that students can listen out for the relevant information.

1   **1 19** The focus on vocabulary lightens the listening load for students and deals with some of the less frequent vocabulary of the text. Ask students to match the words and to predict how they will be used in the talk. Then play the recording for students to check their answers.

Answers
1 economical
2 competent
3 eye-catching
4 crucial
5 appealing
6 promotional
7 well-proportioned
8 lower-case type
9 take something seriously

Today I'd like to talk about how to design a good leaflet. Good design should be eye-catching, attractive, and communicate information effectively and economically.

All groups, whether it's a sports centre, festival organisers or an environmental group, will need to create promotional material at some stage in order to tell people who they are, what they do and to promote their activities. My particular background is in tourism. In order to be taken seriously, groups will expect their material to look professional, competent and to attract attention.

The basic characteristic of all good design for leaflets (and by the way, I'd also include posters and advertisements) is balance. By that, I mean making sure that there's enough white space, and that the layout is even, symmetrical, and well proportioned. A good design will also have movement – that is, it will encourage the reader to move from one point to another – but actually this is less crucial than the first point.

Good use of colour and size of text will help make the most important elements of the information stand out. Recent research shows that font type has a tremendous effect, much more than colour or text size. So ask a friend or colleague to try reading your leaflet to check that it's easy to read. Use upper- and lower-case type appropriately throughout. If you use all upper-case type, it's more difficult and tiring to read.

There are five main elements worth considering in the layout of a leaflet. First, the headline. Don't confuse this with the headings. Place it at the top, using as few words as possible, so that it can be read quickly to grab the reader's interest.

Second, the sub-head. Place this below the headline, creating a short, what I call 'caption', that summarises the key information. This should be in smaller or lighter type.

Third, there's the copy. This is the text and wording containing the main information: who, what, where, when, how much, etc. If you have headings for these, it'll guide the reader through the leaflet.

Fourth, include some sort of image or photo. Choose something clear, bold and appealing because an image is likely to be the first thing that catches your eye. And most importantly, think about it from the perspective of your viewer rather than group organiser or director.

And finally, and it's surprising how often this information is forgotten, you need to include contact details. If these are omitted, no matter how good the rest of the leaflet is, if people can't follow up on the information, you could say everything else was wasted.

Note: make sure students understand that this advice is very useful for real-life situations, but that in an exam situation, they should not spend time on visuals and colour when writing an information text because they are only marked on language.

2   Ask students to listen and write a word they hear to complete the sentences.

Answers

a	tourism	d	caption
b	balance	e	viewer
c	font type	f	contact details

3

Answers

It could appeal to the target reader (students) more. It could be more informal, more encouraging/positive. Encourage students to give other ideas about, for example, the layout.

Extension activity

Extend students' vocabulary by asking them to make posters for the classroom which illustrate vocabulary on the theme of decision-making. Example headings could be: *Life-changing decisions*, *Verbs associated with decision* or *Pictures of different ceremonies* (weddings, etc.) with descriptive texts beneath.

-ing forms

The language here is covered on page 169 of the Grammar folder

1   Students choose the correct verb forms. You could play the recording once more for students to check their answers, to allow them to hear the language in context.

Answers

a	to talk	d	reading
b	making	e	considering
c	make	f	to include

2   Ask students to work with a partner and to match example sentences a–g with uses 1–7.

Answers

a	3	e	4
b	5	f	5 and 7
c	6	g	2 and 5
d	1		

3 Ask students to put the sentences in the correct order, then to underline all the *-ing* forms.

Answers
2 e   3 c   4 f   5 d   6 b

B Travelling
C tending, encouraging
D taking, making
E setting out
F feeling
G waking up, knowing

Corpus spot

Go through the information in the Corpus spot with students. Focus students on the verb forms in each sentence (e.g. *laugh*) and ask whether they are correct.

Answers
1 Some people would probably burst out **laughing**.
2 Our generation has grown up in a society which is used to **having** greater access to information.
3 **Having** a break to doing something different is the best way to solve the problem.
4 I am looking forward to **seeing** you again.
5 ✓
6 It was my fault **not telling** you about our plans. You must have been very puzzled.
7 ✓
8 Technology has affected our lives and will continue **to do** so.

Speaking

1 Ask students to discuss questions a–c in pairs or in small groups. Leave time for whole-class feedback before going on to Exercise 2.

2 The aim here is to get students used to speaking on their own for one minute. Remind students that in the exam, they do not get preparation time but they do have pictures to talk about for one minute. Encourage the student who is listening to give feedback to the speaker. They should say at least one positive thing, give one piece of advice and then say another positive thing. Students should get used to this type of 'feedback sandwich'.

Monitor students as they work and give them a 'feedback sandwich'.

Writing folder 5

Information sheets

1   Ask students to read through the extract from the information sheets and to discuss the questions with a partner.

Answers

A   Parents and children are the intended readers. Strong colours attract attention, especially from children. The different fonts make the information stand out. The colour photo is also eye-catching.

B   Bank customers are the intended readers. The heading with *you* in a box attempts to make customers think that they are important to the bank. The picture of the man on a beach is to make the customer think that his life will be leisurely if he uses the telephone banking service. The tone of the text is also very soothing. The use of a direct question makes the customer feel this new type of banking applies to them.

C   The intended readers are tourists. The leaflet seems to be aimed at those interested in history and the countryside, and uses bullet points to list places of interest.

2   Ask students to choose two or three features they do not expect to find in information sheets.

Answers

jargon, very formal language, long sentences

3   This exercise, together with exercise 4, guides students through the preparation and planning for writing a contribution to an information sheet.

Suggested answers

A   tourists; a contribution to the brochure; what can be done on a countryside holiday; kinds of accommodation; weather conditions

B   visitors to your company; a brief history of the company; main activities; plans for the future; any other points that you think are important

C   a London museum; items of great interest from your country; a contribution to the guide; history of the items, their importance within and outside your country

4   This question provides preparation for writing a contribution to an information sheet.

Suggested answers

Key parts of the question: Your town; visitors; Tourist Board; activities or visits for young people and older people; balance of fun activities and more intellectual activities for the different age ranges

Content: examples of country activities (e.g. sports, parks, walks, wildlife parks, historical places to visit)

Style: welcoming, using lots of adjectives to describe places; informal or neutral language would be suitable

Headings:

Country activities/places

Possible subheading: What to do in the countryside or (name of region)

Information about accommodation

Possible subheading: Where to stay

Information about the weather

Possible subheading: Weather reminder (this will depend on the place and its local climatic conditions)

ⓔxtension activity

If your students would like to choose one of the other writing tasks, you could develop the following.

Task B

This question is easier to answer if you can base your contribution on a real company you know.

Decide on a company you know or a type of company that you could write about. Make sure you have enough information to answer all parts of the question.

The style should be neutral. The main purpose of the information sheet is to give information.

Heading: A description of the origins and past of the company

Possible subheading: A brief history of the company

Heading: A description of the business of the company

Possible subheading: Our product/services

Task C

Include details of historical/cultural items from your country. Remember they must be suitable for a museum in London, so they must be transportable and of interest to museum visitors.

The style should be neutral or formal to reflect the importance of the items.

The introduction should give some background to the items.

Possible heading: Our legacy

Historical details of the items. The origins of (name of items)

The significance of the items in our country and abroad

Possible heading: True treasures

5   Students can write their contributions either in pairs or on their own. Students then exchange their first draft with another student/pair of students.

Encourage students to use the Exam information box as they check each other's writing.

The final draft could be written for homework.

Fact or fantasy

Speaking	Dreaming
Reading and listening	*The Dream*
Grammar	Past tenses and the present perfect
Vocabulary	Adjectives and adjectival order
Speaking	Telling a story

Workbook contents

Use of English	Part 2 – open gap fill
Vocabulary	Evocative adjectives
Reading	Matching extracts to genres; putting jumbled paragraphs into the correct order
Grammar	Past tenses and the present perfect

Student's book pages 82–85

Lesson planning

SV   Grammar exercise 3 could be set for homework.

LV   See the extension activities in the Reading and Listening sections.

Speaking

1   The aim of this exercise is to introduce the topic of dreams. Ask students to work in small groups to discuss the questions. Allow time for class feedback on any interesting points which come up in the discussion.

2   There are no right or wrong answers and students may well have different ideas. Ask them to explain or justify their interpretations.

Reading and listening

1   The text has been labelled as C2 level because it is taken from a short story, written in a rather formal, old-fashioned style. It also uses very literary vocabulary. Ask students to read the first part of the story and then answer the questions with a partner.

Suggested answers

a   He had been advised to travel from New York to Petrograd via Vladivostok as this route would be safer.

b   As the station restaurant was crowded, they were sharing a table at dinner time.

c   He was tall and very fat and he did not look after his clothes. He was well educated, he spoke English well and he could discuss literature.

d   He says he is a journalist, but it is inferred that he wants to keep his real profession secret. He could be a secret agent, a criminal, an undercover police officer or a politician.

2   All the words in this exercise are in the order in which they appear in the story extract. Check whether students would like any other vocabulary explained.

Answers

a   stout   d   shabby
b   paunch   e   tiresome
c   sallow   f   dissimulation

3   This question is open for students to imagine how the story will continue.

4   **2 01** Ask students to listen and get general impressions in answer to questions a–c.

Suggested answers

a   He was talkative, he was of noble birth, a lawyer by profession. He had been in trouble with the 'authorities', so he had had to be abroad a lot. He had been doing business in Vladivostok. He would be in Moscow in a week. He was a widower.

b   She was Swiss and spoke English, German, French and Italian perfectly and good Russian. She had taught languages at one of the best schools in Petrograd.

c   The narrator seems to have found it unusual that the man had told him so much about himself unasked. He felt the man's question about whether he was married was a little too personal. The narrator was wondering, while the man was telling his story, whether he would have time to eat before his train left. The narrator found it laughable that anyone could love the man to distraction, because he found him very ugly.

Recording script

By this time, we had persuaded the waiter to bring us some cabbage soup, and my acquaintance pulled a small bottle of vodka from his pocket which he invited me to share. I do not know whether it was the vodka or the natural loquaciousness of his race that made him communicative, but presently he told me, unasked, a good deal about himself. He was of noble birth, it appeared, a lawyer by profession, and a radical. Some trouble with the authorities had made it necessary for him to be much abroad, but now he was on his way home. Business had detained him at Vladivostok, but he expected to start for Moscow in a week and if I went there, he would be charmed to see me.

'Are you married?' he asked me.

I did not see what business it was of his, but I told him that I was. He sighed a little.

'I am a widower,' he said. 'My wife was a Swiss, a native of Geneva. She was a very cultured woman. She spoke English, German and Italian perfectly. French, of course, was her native tongue. Her Russian was much above the average for a foreigner. She had scarcely the trace of an accent.'

He called a waiter who was passing with a tray full of dishes and asked him, I suppose – for then I knew hardly any Russian – how much longer we were going to wait for the next course. The waiter, with a rapid but presumably reassuring exclamation, hurried on, and my friend sighed.

'Since the revolution the waiting in restaurants has become abominable.'

He lighted his twentieth cigarette and I, looking at my watch, wondered whether I should get a square meal before it was time for me to start.

'My wife was a very remarkable woman,' he continued. 'She taught languages at one of the best schools for the daughters of noblemen in Petrograd. For a good many years we lived together on perfectly friendly terms. She was, however, of a jealous temperament and unfortunately she loved me to distraction.'

It was difficult for me to keep a straight face. He was one of the ugliest men I had ever seen. There is sometimes a certain charm in the rubicund and jovial fat, but this saturnine obesity was repulsive.

5 The significant words are *jealous* and *unfortunately*. These words imply that the Russian might have had to do something drastic about his wife's jealousy.

6 Ask students to work in small groups to speculate about how the story will continue.

7 Students read on and answer the questions.

Answers
1 B   2 C

9

Answers
b The dream could be a kind of omen.
c This question is open to interpretation but students may suggest that the Russian will kill his wife as in her dream.

Extension activity

Students could write the ending to the story in any way they choose before listening to the rest of the recording.

10 **2 02** Ask students to read the questions before they listen, then play the recording.

11 Students compare their answers, using their notes.

Suggested answers
a The man began to think about the dream too. He realised his wife thought he hated her and could be capable of murdering her. When he walked up the stairs it was impossible not to imagine the scene his wife had described in her dream and think about how easy it would be.
b No. He said he wished to be free of her, that she might leave him or die a natural death, but not that he could murder her.
c For a short time, she became less bitter and more tolerant.
d The second dream was the same as the first.
e Perhaps because the memory of the situation was so vivid, or perhaps because he had murdered his wife.
f She had fallen over the baluster and was found dead at the bottom of the stairs by a lodger.
g He seemed nervous, he had a malicious, cunning look and his eyes sparkled.
h Did the man murder her or was it an accident? We do not know for sure but this is the narrator's suspicion or nagging doubt.

'She was much shaken. I did my best to soothe her. But next morning, and for two or three days after, she referred to the subject again and, notwithstanding my laughter, I saw that it dwelt in her mind. I could not help thinking of it either, for this dream showed me something that I had never suspected. She thought I hated her, she thought I would gladly be rid of her, she knew of course that she was insufferable, and at some time or other the idea had evidently occurred to her that I was capable of murdering her. The thoughts of men are incalculable and ideas enter our minds that we should be ashamed to confess. Sometimes I had wished she might run away with a lover, sometimes that a painless and sudden death might give me my freedom, but never had the idea come to me that I might deliberately rid myself of an intolerable burden.

'The dream made an extraordinary impression upon both of us. It frightened my wife, and she became for a while a little less bitter and more tolerant. But when I walked up the stairs to our apartment it was impossible for me not to look over the balusters and reflect how easy it would be to do what she had dreamed. The balusters were dangerously low. A quick gesture and the thing was done. It was hard to put the thought out of my mind. Then some months later my wife awakened me one night. I was very tired and I was exasperated. She was white and trembling. She had had the dream again. She burst into tears and asked me if I hated her. I swore by all the saints of the Russian calendar that I loved her. At last she went to sleep again. It was more than I could do. I lay awake. I seemed to see her falling down the well of the stairs, and I heard a shriek and the thud as she struck the stone floor. I could not help shivering.'

The Russian stopped and beads of sweat stood on his forehead. He had told the story well and fluently so that I had listened with attention. There was still some vodka in the bottle, he poured it out and swallowed it at a gulp.

'And how did your wife eventually die?' I asked after a pause.

He took out a dirty handkerchief and wiped his forehead.

'By an extraordinary coincidence she was found late one night at the bottom of the stairs with her neck broken.'

'Who found her?'

'She was found by one of the lodgers who came in shortly after the catastrophe.'

'And where were you?'

I cannot describe the look he gave me of malicious cunning. His little black eyes sparkled.

'I was spending the evening with a friend of mine. I did not come in till an hour later.'

At that moment the waiter brought us the dish of meat that we had ordered, and the Russian fell upon it with good appetite. He shovelled the food into his mouth in enormous mouthfuls.

I was taken aback. Had he really been telling me in this hardly veiled manner that he had murdered his wife? That obese and sluggish man did not look like a murderer, I could not believe that he would have had the courage. Or was he making a sardonic joke at my expense?

In a few minutes it was time for me to go and catch my train. I left him and have not seen him since. But I have never been able to make up my mind whether he was serious or jesting.

12 Divide your class into small groups so that they can discuss this. Feed back the main ideas at the end with the whole class.

Past tenses and the present perfect

The language here is covered on page 169 of the Grammar folder.

1 The aim is to revise and extend students' knowledge and use of past tenses and the present perfect.

Answers
He called a waiter who was passing with a tray full of dishes and asked him, I suppose – for then I hardly knew any Russian – how much longer we were going to wait for the next course. The waiter, with a rapid but presumably reassuring exclamation, hurried on, and my friend sighed.

2 Elicit the information in the Grammar Folder on page 169.

3 This exercise could be set for homework if time is short.

Answers
a I'd read many other stories by this author before I read *The Dream*.
b ✓
c The short story was made into a TV drama last year.
d The author owned an interesting collection of antiquarian books.
e ✓
f ✓
g ✓
h ✓
i ✓
j The first page of the book didn't seem very interesting, that's why I didn't read it.
k He had been writing for magazines for years before he was discovered by Hollywood.
l ✓
m Are you sure the man committed the murder? I thought it was the lodger.

4 Students should use the present perfect simple or continuous in response to the pictures.

Suggested answers
B She has just hit the ball.
C She's had her hair cut. / She's been to the salon.
D He's done something wrong.
E They've been running for three hours. / They've finished the race.
F He's forgotten her name.
G It's finished the food. / It's been eating its dinner.
H They have just arrived. / They've been travelling.
I He's been working in a garage. / He's fixed the car.

5 Go through the information in the Corpus spot before asking students to do the exercise.

Answers
a has been writing
b have been going
c haven't used
d has always been
e have been playing

Vocabulary

Establish the usual order of adjectives by going through the Vocabulary spot.

1 Ask students to put the adjectives in the most usual order.

Answers
a a small wooden table
b an exciting, extensive new menu
c a beautiful red silk dress
d a shabby black suit
e a huge sallow face

2 Make sure students understand the words in the box. You could ask them to show examples of the words in the photos. Accept any appropriate answers from students. Encourage them to use a variety of adjectives.

Speaking

1 Go through the introduction to this section. Monitor students as they work in pairs to prepare their stories. Encourage them to use descriptive vocabulary and a range of past tenses in their stories. If students want to be imaginative, encourage them.

After the preparation time, ask students to take turns to tell their stories to another pair. As a round-up, ask students to talk about the stories they enjoyed hearing. Students could write up their stories for homework.

Exam folder 6

Student's book pages 86–87
Paper 1 Part 1 Themed texts

Go through the introduction to this folder.

1 Ask students to read the first extract and answer the questions.

Answers
a There was something in the stance or movement of the accompanist and the woman that strongly suggested that they were about to kiss.
b A musical event, because the word *accompanist* suggests a musician accompanying a singer.

2 Remind students that focusing on the question rather than the options is a good way to train yourself to find the correct answer to multiple-choice questions.

Answers
1 D   **2** A

3

Answers
3 C   **4** A

4 Make the point that students should always be able to justify their choices by identifying exactly where the answer is in the review.

Answers
Alastair Marriott, whose new work 'Kiss' was created for her, understands this, giving her the chance to take the dance in completely unexpected directions. Her limbs are graceful, her legs seem to unfold in a swelling legato, her back melts at the very touch of air – Bussell is big, her dance is big and Marriott has offered her choreography which is undoubtedly big in gesture. Yet somehow it seems to be at odds with the theme of the ballet, which is inspired by the quiet and intimate love of the sculptor Auguste Rodin and his muse Camille Claudel ...

5 Ask students to check all the points in the Exam information box on page 86 before you confirm the correct answers.

Answers
5 C   **6** A

14 Evolving language

GENRE: Lectures
TOPIC: Human communication

Listening	Types of speech; a lecture
Reading	An essay
Grammar	The passive; *to have/get something done*
Vocabulary	Word formation
Speaking	Giving a talk

Workbook contents

Vocabulary	Phrases with *talk*
Grammar	The passive
Listening	A lecture
Writing	Reviewing a lecture

Student's book pages 88–89

Lesson planning

SV Grammar exercises 3 and 5 could be set for homework.

LV See the extension activity in the Reading section.

Listening

1 Ask students to look at the photos and discuss what the situation is, who is talking, and what type of speech is being given.

2 **2 03**

Answers
1 c 2 d 3 b 4 a

Recording script

Speaker 1: Now we have, over the last four days, heard that the goods were taken from the warehouse on the night of February 14th. The theft was discovered by Mr White when he arrived on the morning of February 15th. There was overwhelming forensic evidence which puts Geoff Warren in the frame. His fingerprints were found on the window along with fibres from his jacket. Later, some of our officers found some of the goods at his home address in Germaine Street.

Speaker 2: So, to recap, it was announced by the prime minister this morning that the general election will be held on May 3rd. The election campaign is to start with immediate effect with the three main parties having air time on both TV and radio over the

coming weeks. So, with that I will take your questions. Yes – Ben Palmer, Associated News – you first.

Speaker 3: Jill Davies will be remembered both as devoted mother and wife and also for her work at St Thomas's hospital, where she worked as a paediatrician for many years. She will remain in the hearts of all those who knew her, even though her body may have departed this world. Her pioneering work has meant that many more families have had the joy of taking home their newborn. The procedures she introduced are now an established part of hospital life.

Speaker 4: We can see in our communities many who are in need, and the parable of the Good Samaritan teaches us that we should not pass by those in need. Those who, for whatever reason, cross our path in our daily life, and are less fortunate than ourselves, should be shown true compassion. Even the smallest gesture, such as listening for a few extra minutes to someone who has a problem, can make all the difference.

3 Students should work with a partner to match the words to the definitions.

Answers
a a briefing c a presentation
b a lecture d a seminar

Go through the Exam spot so that students can appreciate the relevance of the class work to the exam.

4 The aim of this pre-listening exercise is to introduce some of the topics in the listening and so make the exercises more accessible. Do not go through the answers until students have done the listening as well as the reading in the next section.

Answers
1 A or B 3 B
2 B 4 C

5 **2 04** Encourage students to look at the questions before you play the recording.

Answers
a 6,000 e gestures
b 9,000; 1.3 million f primitive; basic; natural
c 1.5 million years g tools; at night (time)
d 300,000

Recording script

In this lecture on the evolutionary factors of language, I'm going to begin by looking at early language in humans.

Writing began about 6,000 years ago, so it is fair to say that speech preceded that, although estimates of when humans began to speak range from 9,000 years ago to 1.3 million years ago. Primitive tools have been found that date back to 1.5 million years BC – the tools show that our ancestors had at least low-level spatial thinking. Later tools, about 300,000 years old, are more advanced, revealing that cognition was on a level that was similar or equal to modern intelligence – tools had been planned in three dimensions, allowing for abstract thought – the cognitive capacity for language was present.

Krantz (1980) argues that language emerged 50,000 years ago because then the fossil records show that significant changes took place. Tools became more sophisticated and specialised, projectiles appeared along with fire and there was a large spread and expansion of the population. According to Krantz, the cause may have been to do with the emergence of full language and a new cognitive competence in humans.

Presumably, initially, people used gestures to communicate, then gestures with vocal communication. Both provided an evolutionary push towards a higher level of cognition, fuelled by a need to communicate effectively and the frustration at not being able to do so. Pettito and Marentette (1991) examined deaf infants, and found that they start to babble, and then because there is no auditory feedback, they stop. Deaf children use manual babbling (an early form of sign language equivalent to the vocalisations of hearing infants) but this manual babbling stage starts earlier than in hearing children and ends sooner. Pettito and Marentette suggest that manual language is therefore more primitive, basic and natural than spoken language, a clue that the first languages were iconic, not spoken.

The emergence of tool use with spoken language is particularly interesting. Possibly, hands were needed to manipulate tools, and humans found it difficult to communicate with sign language and use tools at the same time. Vocal communication, if possible, would allow the hands to do other things. Also, a vocal language would allow humans to communicate at night-time, and without having to look at each other.

Reading

1 Allow students time to read the extract from an essay on their own. Tell them not to worry about unknown vocabulary at this stage. Then ask them to work with a partner and answer the questions.

Answers
1 B   2 C   3 A

Extension activity

Make a matching exercise for any unknown vocabulary from the essay that your students might like to explore. Write definitions of the unknown words on the board and get students to match them to words or phrases in the essay.

2 Allow time for a discussion to round off the Reading section.

The passive

The language here is covered on page 171 of the Grammar folder.

1 If you consider it necessary, also ask your students how the passive is formed (to be + past participle).

Answer
It is common for the passive to be used in statements like this when the action is more important than the person who carried it out. The passive is also commonly used when we do not know who did something.

2 This exercise serves as revision and expansion of the use of the passive.

Answers
1 e   2 h   3 b   4 i   5 g   6 d   7 c   8 a   9 f

3 The continuous text will help students think about whether it is suitable to turn a sentence into the passive or not. Obviously, not every sentence would usually be in the passive in a text.

4 Go through the Corpus spot and encourage students to take care when using the passive in exercise 4.

Suggested answers

The vase has been stolen.
The TV and DVD player have been stolen.
The chair has been moved nearer to the fireplace.
The carpet has been moved.
The camera has been put on the floor.
The sofa cushion has been moved.
The photo has been dropped on the floor.
A lampshade has been broken.
The windows have been opened.
A window blind has been pulled down.

5

Answers

a The new court house is being constructed/built.
b The proposals have been considered by the board.
c The situation is now being controlled.
d I was ordered not to divulge the company's future plans.
e The prime minister was attacked for the statements he made.

6 Refer to the Grammar folder on page 171 for the explanations to these questions.

7

Answers

a Have you ever had
b had our wedding photos taken by
c to have/get a special ring made

Vocabulary

Teaching extra

Whenever possible, elicit or give the different forms of words when students meet new vocabulary. Develop this habit in students.

1 Refer students to the Vocabulary spot. Ask students to read the whole text first before they begin to write the words so that they understand it. Remind students to check which part of speech is required in the sentence. Students work on their own first and then compare their answers with a partner.

Elicit the correct answers from the class and ask students to write the words up on the board so that the spelling can be checked.

Answers

1	overlooked	5	excellent
2	underpractised	6	scientific
3	introductory	7	relatively
4	reference	8	memorable

Speaking

1 Go through the instructions. Put students into groups of three (A, B and C) and ask them to go to the relevant page. They read their information. At this point, students should not say aloud which piece of information is correct.

2 Regroup students so that each group of three has one student A, one student B and one student C. Ask students to give their talk based on the notes on the card while the other two students listen out for the piece of information they think is incorrect.

3 Get feedback from the whole class. Ask students to tell each other which piece of information was incorrect. Did they guess correctly?

Writing folder 6

Student's book pages 92–93

Essays

You might like to introduce this Writing folder by asking your students to think of examples of school/academic essays they have written where they had to express their opinion and argue a case.

1   In order to help students to plan essays, first look at the *Content* column of the table, explaining that this is what is typically included at each stage of an essay.

2   Ask students, in pairs, to choose from the list of purposes and write them in the appropriate place in the *Purpose* column.

3   In the table, students should tick the purposes that have been included in the sample essay.

Answers

Stage of essay	Content	Purpose
Introduction	General statement	(1) To introduce the reader to the topic ✓
	Definition(s) – optional	(2) To explain what is understood by some key words/concepts
	Scope of essay	(3) To tell the reader what you intend to cover in this essay ✓
Body	Arguments	(4) To express important ideas ✓
	Evidence	(5) To support ideas with examples ✓
Conclusions	Summary	(6) To remind the reader of the key ideas ✓
	Relate the argument to a more general world view	(7) To underline the writer's point of view ✓

4   Highlight the importance of using connecting words in writing (and speaking): they act as signposts for the reader so that he/she can follow the line of argument.

Answers
while, On the one hand, In addition, for example, On the other hand, and, the like, because, and, In my opinion, Moreover
Note: most of the linkers are formal – *and* and *because* are less formal.
On the one/other hand, In addition, for example, In my opinion and *Moreover* are followed by a comma.

5   Students could work in small groups straightaway to complete the table or you could work with the class as a whole, eliciting some ideas and writing them up on the board. You could then let students work in small groups to complete the table.

Suggested answers
a my teacher   **b** formal   **c** 250 words

	Content	Purpose
Introduction	• More people are studying English • English, Spanish, Chinese as world language? • Discuss ways in which it will be easier • Examine what problems there might be	(1) To introduce the reader to the topic (2) To tell the reader what you intend to cover in this essay
Body	For one language Everyone learns at young age – easy (e.g. bilingual children) Travel: easier to make arrangements, get help, get info, meet people Study: easier to follow any course, anywhere (but not always possible) Better job prospects <u>Might lose:</u> Cultural identity, thrill of travel	(3) To express important ideas (4) To support ideas with examples
Conclusion	Many activities will be easier but keep cultural identity / traditions	(5) To remind the reader of key ideas (6) To underline my point of view

6   Ask students to work in pairs or small groups to brainstorm vocabulary. When they have finished, get feedback from the whole class. Write their suggestions on the board to create a list of vocabulary and key phrases. Explain the meaning of any unknown phrases.

7   Ask students to work in pairs or small groups to discuss any further tips. Once again, write whole-class suggestions on the board.

8   Students write their essay individually or for homework. Encourage them to use the vocabulary and the tips you all discussed. When they have finished, pairs could exchange their writing and feed back on how well they followed the tips for essay writing outlined in exercise 7.

15 In my view ...

GENRE: Expressing opinions
TOPIC: Family life

Speaking and Reading	Family life
Vocabulary	Agreeing and disagreeing
Grammar	The infinitive
Listening	TV programmes
Workbook contents	
Reading	Putting paragraphs into gaps
Vocabulary	Guessing meaning from context
Grammar	The infinitive

Student's book pages 94–97

Lesson planning
SV Grammar exercise 2 could be set for homework.
LV See extension activities in the Speaking and Reading section.

Speaking and Reading

Establish that the theme of the unit is expressing opinions by asking when the phrase *In my view ...* could be used.

1 Ask students to match the photographs to the speakers.

Answers
1 A   2 D   3 B   4 C

2 Ask students to continue to work in pairs and to match the synonyms.

Answers
a 3   b 5   c 6   d 2   e 4   f 1

3 Students discuss the two questions. Raise awareness of the language we use when we want to be forceful (or tactful/kind/sensitive).

Elicit from students the different ways that people use to air their opinions (e.g. newspaper articles, speeches, letters to magazines/newspapers, radio phone-in programmes, internet forums, blogs, Twitter feeds and social-networking sites).

4 Encourage students to look at the title of the article and to speculate about what might be included in it. Possible suggestions could be issues to do with manners, behaviour, staying out late, spending too much money, doing homework, helping in the house, etc. You could also elicit what sort of punishments parents impose on children when children have done something wrong.

5 Ask students to read the whole article, then read the questions and choose the best answer, A, B, C or D.

Answers
1 B   2 D   3 C   4 A   5 C

Extension activity

Ask students to go through the article and underline Jonathan's opinions. Then ask students to go through each one and discuss whether they agree or disagree with them.
- *I think children want to feel proud of their parents because it makes them feel secure in a Darwinian sense.*
- *I have inherited from my father a strong sense of the importance of doing the right thing.*
- *I believe strongly in proper bedtimes, that chores have to be done and that certain times of the day are reserved for adults.*
- *I want to make my children into the sort of children I want them to be.*
- *We live in a terribly liberal age when people feel they should take a back seat in making moral decisions.*
- *I don't believe in reasoning with my children.*
- *I can't stand all those Saturday morning programmes.*
- *I think it's a parent's job to preserve childhood as long as possible.*
- *I am strict about homework and achievement. Our children will work hard until they finish university and I think they will thank me for the rest of their lives.*
- *I don't like the attitudes in football.*

Vocabulary

1 Ask students to think back to the article and say whether they agree or disagree with the opinions expressed in it. Point out the range of functions for agreeing and disagreeing.

2 Students rank the ideas, saying which ones are most important, and supporting their views with reasons.

3 Round off with this personalisation task.

Go through the Exam spot. It is important that students interact together in Part 3 of the Speaking test (Paper 5). They will be expected to contribute fully to the task and to develop the interaction. They should also be sensitive to turn-taking and should neither dominate nor give only minimal responses.

4   Go through the selection of phrases for starting off Part 3 of the Speaking test and decide which ones are appropriate.

Answers
2, 4, 5, 8

Encourage students to practise giving their opinions, using some of the language worked on in this unit.

Extension activity

Make posters of different functions under different categories, which students can use when discussing their opinions.

Inviting opinions
What do you think?
Do you agree?
And you?
What about you?

Giving an opinion
I think ...
As far as I know ...
Well, in my opinion ...

Justifying an opinion
because
so
since

5   This serves as a reminder that students should use the phrases they have just worked on to practise for Part 3 of the Speaking test (Paper 5).

The infinitive

The language here is covered on page 171 of the Grammar folder. Go through the introduction to this section, checking that students understand.

1   Ask students to look for some examples of the infinitive with and without *to* in the reading text.

Answers
Infinitive with *to*: a, c
Infinitive without *to*: b, d

2   Go through the Corpus spot and encourage students to take care when doing exercise 2. This exercise could be set for homework. Point out that some of the sentences need no corrections.

Answers
a   I don't want you **to** think I'm complaining, because I am not.
b   ✓
c   I must **to go** home before I miss the last bus.
d   In my opinion parents should not let their daughters **to wear** make-up until they are over 16.
e   ✓
f   ✓
g   ✓
h   It was fantastic **to** see so many young people enter the competition.
i   ✓

Listening

1   Students should work with a partner or in small groups to discuss these pre-listening questions.

2   **2 05** Go through the instructions for the listening task. As they listen, students match the speakers to the programmes. This is the same task type as in the Listening test (Paper 4) Part 4.

Answers
B, C, E, G, H

3   **2 05** Play the recording again.

Answers
A, C, D, F, G

4   A discussion in small groups will round off the unit.

Recording script

Karim: Did you see that show last night?

Stella: Which one?

Karim: At 9.30, after the news.

Claire: Oh yeah, I saw it. It was like *I Love the Eighties*. I enjoyed that.

Karim: Well, I'm not old enough to remember the 80s, but …

Claire: Hey!

Stella: I mean, sorry, I wanted to say I did most of my growing up in the 90s, so this show last night … it brought back loads of memories. It was done really well, too. Old TV clips, adverts, music, everything. Really took me back to my childhood.

Stella: No, I didn't watch that. I was watching the other channel. It was a documentary by the same people who did *Predators*.

Karim: What, the nature documentary? With the CGI effects?

Stella: That's the one. Well, they've made this new documentary, where they bring prehistoric times to life. The special effects are just so impressive, and real. Huw Baker does the commentary on it. He does it really tongue-in-cheek, which is good because it gets a lot of information across, and it's really fun. Anyone can understand.

Karim: Even you.

Stella: Even me, yes.

Claire: I haven't seen any good documentaries recently. There was this really stupid one. I can't remember, maybe last week. I normally like anything about history, but I sat down to watch it and … It was supposed to be about England and the monarchy five hundred years ago, right? And they just had modern music in the background.

Karim: That's OK, isn't it?

Claire: Yes, but that period boasted some of England's finest music, so why couldn't some of it have found its way into this programme? After all, we know what music was performed at the great state occasions of the time and yeah, there are probably lots of performers who could have done it justice.

Karim: They really know how to ruin some programmes, don't they? You know, when my favourite TV show came back …

Claire: Oh, not that stupid cookery show.

Karim: It's not stupid! Well, it didn't use to be. But they changed it. Now it's all about the celebrities more than anything else, now. The recipes look great but why can't they just show them preparing the dishes? What's wrong with that? Now they've tried to make it into some kind of competition. Will they get it cooked on time? Who will be the winner? There's always something distracting the viewer from what's going on, as if we've got no attention span at all!

Claire: Sorry, but I can't stand cookery shows. Why would you want to watch someone cooking? On TV? It's not as if we can taste it, or smell how good they say it is. Anyway, there's almost nothing good on TV these days. Just celebrities and cookery, and reality TV.

Karim: Yeah, I wouldn't miss reality TV shows if they completely disappeared.

Stella: Actually, I don't like reality shows. I'm not interested in who the latest pop star's going to be, or whether someone's going to survive another week locked up in a house. But this one now on Saturdays, it's wonderful …

Claire: What, the one with the singing housewives and talking dogs? You can't be serious?

Stella: I'm really starting to get into it! I think it's because they're just ordinary people. Well, I say ordinary, some of them are really gifted. Like the woman they had on last week. She had an amazing singing voice. I want to see if she gets voted off next week.

Claire: I'm shocked …

Stella: No, watch it, it's great!

Units 11–15 Revision

Student's book pages 98–99

Topic review

Ask students to work with a partner to discuss questions a–j. The aim of this exercise is to encourage students to recycle the vocabulary and structures they have covered in the preceding units in a personalised way.

Reading

1 Ask students to read the article and to answer questions 1–3. They should compare their answers in pairs before you check the answers.

Answers
1 C   2 C   3 B

Grammar

1 This tests students' knowledge of the use of the infinitive with and without *to* as well as the *-ing* form.

Answers
1 to be
2 to fetch
3 lying
4 to remain
5 to say
6 flocking
7 to find
8 to stand up
9 to secure
10 complaining

Speaking

1 Although one aim of this exercise is for students to practise the grammar points listed in the rubric, be flexible about this. Allowing students to take stock of their progress is equally important.

2 Encourage students to change places in the room and interview each other. After they have interviewed each other, allow time for discussion of anything the students want to bring up regarding their course.

Vocabulary

1 Ask students first to identify the missing part of speech and then to work on their own to fill the gaps.

Answers
1 concentration
2 inability
3 laziness
4 developing
5 adulthood
6 younger
7 activity
8 environmental

16 What if ... ?

GENRE: Competition entries
TOPIC: Mini sagas

Speaking	Talking about competitions
Reading	Mini sagas
Vocabulary	Idioms of the body
Grammar	Hypothesising
Workbook contents	
Grammar	Hypothesising
Vocabulary	Idioms of the body
Use of English	Part 2 – open gap fill
Listening	Mini sagas

Student's book pages 100–103

Lesson planning

SV Reading exercise 2 and Vocabulary exercise 3 could be set for homework.

LV See the extension activity in the Grammar section.

Speaking

When introducing this unit, point out to students that the Writing test (Paper 2) often asks students to write a competition entry. Elicit from students that a competition entry tries particularly hard to be interesting and original and to engage the reader.

1   Students discuss questions a–c with a partner. They should then feed back to the class about any competitions they themselves have entered.

2   Students work with a partner to discuss questions a and b and then compare their answers with the rest of the class.

Reading

Students are not asked to read or write a mini saga in the exam but these are focused on here as they show interesting use of language and how to be economical with writing and pay attention to word limits.

1   Students should read the mini sagas and match the titles with the sagas.

Answers
1 D   2 C   3 A   4 B   5 E

2   The words and expressions in this exercise are in the order in which they occur in the mini sagas. Ask students to match them to the meanings given as quickly as possible.

Answers
exceptionally good = *outstanding*
using words in a clever and humorous way = *witty*
a work of art = *a masterpiece*
conspiracy = *plot*
infection = *bug*
treat a weaker person in a cruel way = *bully*
try to keep cheerful = *chin up*
improve = *enhance*
bankrupt = *bust*
thinking about something else = *distracted*

3   There are no precise answers to this question but discussing it should help students to focus on the meaning of what each saga is about.

Suggested answers
B Don't make up your mind until you know the whole story.
C Treat your children well as it will affect how they treat you in your old age.
D Don't put your trust in modern management techniques.
E Pay attention to what is important.

4   Divide students into small groups to discuss this question. It may be of interest to them to know that the winner of the competition was *Like Mother, Like Son*.

Vocabulary

1 As a lead in, ask students if they can name any other idioms that are based on parts of the body.

Students do exercise 1 with a partner. Ask them also to be prepared to explain what each of the idioms means. They may use an English–English dictionary if necessary. Online help is available at http://dictionaries.cambridge.org/

Answers
1	E (finger)	5	H (ears)
2	I (toes)	6	A (head)
3	D (heart)	7	G (feet)
4	B (hand)	8	F (eye)

2 Students do this exercise in pairs. They can use an English–English dictionary if necessary.

Answers
a 5   b 7   c 4   d 1   e 8   f 2   g 3   h 6

3 This exercise helps students to contextualise some of the idioms they have been working on.

Answers
1 fell head over heels in love
2 to give her a hand
3 has her head in the clouds
4 has set her heart
5 keeps her on her toes
6 was all ears
7 bite his tongue
8 was down in the mouth
9 is breaking my heart
10 racked my brains
11 put his mind at rest
12 to keep my fingers crossed

Hypothesising

The language here is covered on page 172 of the Grammar folder. Refer students to the Exam spot before drawing their attention to the examples.

1 The aim of the introductory question is to focus on register. Do it with the class as a whole. Elicit the fact that shorter expressions tend to be less formal than longer ones. Longer, more formal expressions often contain examples of modal verbs (*may*), inversion (*Were we to …*; *Had we*) and begin with a participle phrase (*Provided …*; *Given …*; *Had we …*).

Answers
1 B   2 A

Extension activity

Ask students to create sentences using some of the examples in the boxes to talk about the following situations:
• what they would do if they won a large amount of money.
• what they would do if a friend suggested that they should both give up their jobs and travel round the world together.
• what they would do if they could have three wishes come true.

2 **2 06** Play the recording. Students listen and tick any of the expressions from box A that they hear.

Recording script
Kate: Why don't we enter this competition? The first prize is a holiday for two. Just imagine if we won! I'd love to go on holiday.
Tom: Me too. So, we have to write a 250-word article about a holiday. What if we each do an article? Then we'd have twice as much chance of winning.
Kate: OK. I wonder if it would be better to write something serious and clever or something more fun?
Tom: I don't know. If only we had more information about what the judges are going to be looking for.
Kate: Well, suppose you send in something funny and I'll try something more serious. Then perhaps one of us will hit the note they want.
Tom: OK, so now let's …

Answers
All the expressions in box A are used. These are the ones which are most likely to be used when hypothesising in relatively informal situations.

Corpus spot

Go through the information in the Corpus spot. Focus students on the phrases used for hypothesising, and the structures of the verb forms.

Answers
1 I was wondering **whether / if** you could make it in July?
2 Imagine **you had** to live with no central heating …
3 Suppose she **took** the job in Moscow, how **would we** manage without her? / Suppose she **takes** the job in Moscow, how **will** we manage without her?
4 The best way to prepare yourself for the driving test is to **imagine** yourself as a driver.

3   Students prepare these sentences, then check their answers with the whole class.

Answers
1   a   If we were to each read all the entries and choose our individual three preferences before any group discussion, that would save some time.
    b   Were we to each read all the entries and choose our individual three preferences before any group discussion, that would save some time.
2   a   If we had given competitors more guidance, it'd have helped (them).
    b   Had we given competitors more guidance, that'd have helped them.
3   a   Let us imagine the different kinds of criteria we might be guided by.
    b   Let us consider the different kinds of criteria we might be guided by.
4   a   Let us suppose that most competitors will write about their own experiences.
    b   Let us assume that most competitors will write about their own experiences.

4   **2 07** Students listen to the speech once and discuss the questions with a partner.

Answers
The speaker is arguing that class sizes at primary school should be no larger than 20 pupils. The points are:
•   it will become easier to attract good quality teachers
•   pupils will enjoy school more and there will be fewer discipline problems
•   children will learn more quickly, which will benefit society
•   if enough teachers can be found, the policy can be implemented within five years
•   building budgets for schools will have to be increased
•   the fact that the birth rate has fallen will make it easier to implement the policy than it might otherwise have been.

5   The (mostly formal) phrases for hypothesising are underlined in the script.

Recording script
I am proposing that class sizes at primary school be reduced to a maximum of 20 pupils.

If I may speculate for a moment, I believe that it will be much easier to attract good-quality graduates into the teaching profession if they're guaranteed an environment in which they can truly teach each individual child. Speculating further for a moment, children will enjoy school far more and there will be fewer problems of alienation and truancy among young people.

Let us take a hypothetical case: a rather shy child starts school at four and a half. He is in a class with 36 other children. The teacher never seems to notice when he has trouble understanding the lesson and he gets into the habit of not bothering about being able to keep up with the work. He soon learns that the one way to get attention is to be disruptive.

On the assumption that children learn more, faster and with greater enjoyment if they are in smaller groups with more individual attention, I have every reason to suppose that the implementation of this proposal would have far-reaching benefits for the future of our society.

Provided that we are able to find enough appropriately talented and suitably qualified primary school teachers, I think that there is no reason why the proposal should not be implemented throughout the country within the next five years. Allowing for the fact that more classrooms will be required if class sizes are to be reduced, we shall have to increase schools' building budgets for the next couple of years. Given that the birth rate has fallen over recent years, it should be more straightforward to implement this proposal now than it would have been ten years ago.

6   Ask students to individually think of a law they would like to pass. It doesn't need to be connected with education. If students are having problems with this, you could brainstorm ideas with the whole class and write ideas on the board. Students could then choose one of the laws they find interesting. Give them around five minutes to make notes about the law they chose and language they can use to express their ideas.

7   Put students in small groups to discuss their laws. Go round and monitor that students are using hypothesising language appropriately, and encourage them to ask each other questions.

Exam folder 7

Student's book pages 104–105

Paper 1 Part 2 Gapped text

1   Students do this exercise either in class or at home if time is short.

2   Encourage students to identify the words and phrases which help them fit the paragraphs into the gaps.

Answers
1 C   2 D   3 F   4 E   5 G   6 A

Go through the Exam information box and ask students to discuss why each point is a sensible piece of advice.

17 Rave reviews

GENRE: Reviews
TOPIC: The arts

Speaking	Rave reviews
Reading	Reviews
Vocabulary	Giving opinions
Grammar	Articles
Listening	Discussing films

Workbook contents

Reading	Four reviews
Writing	A review
Use of English	Part 4 – multiple meanings
Grammar	Articles

Student's book pages 106–109

Lesson planning

SV Listening exercises 4 and 5 could be given for homework.

LV See extension activities in the Vocabulary, Grammar and Listening sections.

Speaking

1 Students discuss the questions in pairs. When they have finished, feed back quickly with the whole class.

Reading

1 This reading section has been labelled with a C2-level icon. Some of the reviews contain very sophisticated, vivid language, where the writer is fully able to express his or her views. Students work with a partner to answer the questions. Then they quickly check their answers by scanning the five review extracts.

Suggested answers

A Hostel for backpackers – not clear from the heading if it is going to be mainly praising or criticising.

B It is about a film, although that is not clear from the headline. The headline does, however, make it clear that it is praising rather than criticising.

C It is about a computer game – praising.

D A music album – sounds generally positive but headline does not give much away.

E It is about a website, although the headline only makes clear that it is something digital. It sounds generally as if it is praising rather than criticising – it implies that the website is convenient.

2 This exercise contains three statements about each of the reviews. Ask students to read each review in more detail and decide whether each statement is true, false or if the information is not given in the extracts.

Answers

Review A
a true
b false (the author says it is 'interesting' and 'quirky')
c not given

Review B
a true
b false (it is said to stand up remarkably well)
c not given

Review C
a false (it is the second version)
b false (it is said to be well ahead of previous versions in terms of presentation, structure and accessibility)
c false (the writer says that earlier versions were unforgiving at times, which implies that he or she felt that some improvement would be desirable)

Review D
a true
b not given
c false (it is said to leave the listener with a sense of haunted mystification)

Review E
a true
b not given
c false (the writer says it is easy to explore the site)

Vocabulary

1 This section deals with the language of opinion and suggestion.

Students discuss in pairs whether the phrases are used positively or negatively in the reviews. Discuss the answers with the whole class.

Answers
sleek – positive
quirky – positive
buzzing – positive
palpable – positive
well ahead – positive
unforgiving – negative
gives more leeway – positive
haunted – positive (though this could be negative in other contexts)
embrace – positive
masterpiece – positive
tidy – positive
seamlessly integrated – positive
hit on a formula – positive here (though could be negative in other contexts)

2 This exercise could be done as homework as a way of revising the language in the texts.

Suggested answers
A **positive:** distinctive, architecturally interesting, a pleasant indoor/outdoor feel, hip, helpful
B **positive:** strength and power, truly great, stands up remarkably well, ring true, has lost none of its wit and cleverness, enhanced, perfectly acted, three-dimensional
  negative: horribly dated
C **positive:** has some time for
D **positive:** triumph
E **positive:** popular, easy to browse, well-written, other particularly popular, lots of great stuff to enjoy

3 Students could discuss the exercise with a partner before checking their answers with the class as a whole. Make sure that students learn the whole expression in each sentence.

Answers
a Why **don't** we
b I might as **well**
c am I **right** in saying
d In other **words**
e mainly a **matter** of
f I'm not entirely **convinced**
g I agree with you on the **whole**; **take** you up on
h I'm in two **minds** as to whether

4 This exercise focuses students' attention on the fact that there are fixed collocations which should be learnt as chunks. Divide students into groups of three to five. Encourage them to use some of the expressions from the previous exercise. Allow groups about ten minutes to discuss their plans. They should write notes rather than starting to write a full review. One person from each group should feed back to the class as a whole. Alternatively, students could be put into new groups of three to five so that the original groups are represented in each new group. Feedback could then be done within the new groups. This would have the advantage of involving all the students directly in the feedback process. Students could write the reviews they planned for homework.

Extension activity

Students work in groups of three. They are going to prepare and record a radio review.
- They discuss what they are going to review. It could be a music album, a DVD, a computer game, a school concert, a local café or a sports event. They should be advised to choose something that everyone in the group is familiar with.
- They share their opinions about what they are going to review. What do they each like and dislike about it?
- They discuss how best to present their review for the other students in the class. How much information do they need to include about the subject? How can they make the review more interesting for the listeners?
- Record the review, then play it for other students to listen to.

Articles

The language here is covered on page 172 of the Grammar folder. This section has also been labelled with a C2-level icon. Students are asked to look in detail at sometimes very subtle and sophisticated article use in relation to the five reviews.

1 These questions highlight some of the key points about the use of articles and determiners in English.

Answers
Review A

a No, it couldn't because it is referring to a specific colour which has already been mentioned).

b No, although it might suggest to the reader that there is another kitchen elsewhere.

c Yes, it would then appear to be talking about some specific previously mentioned travellers rather than travellers in general.

Review B

a the truly great film (it's making a general statement)

b viewers

c its themes of courage

Review C

a through a stroke of luck

b a bit of time for

Review D

a listeners

Review E

a No, because Music, Cinema and Home Cinema are referring to general categories rather than to specific examples of music, cinema and home cinema.

b *post any comments*

Corpus spot

Article use is a very common area of error for students at this level. Go through the sentences in the Corpus spot, asking students to focus on misused or missing articles. Encourage students to give reasons for their answers.

Answers

1 **Life** after the revolution was very difficult. (No article is usually used in general statements.)

2 **The** life of an artist or singer is very cruel, full of obstacles and enemies. (The article is used in general statements where the noun has a post-modifying phrase.)

3 My brother is **a** biochemist in London. (The indefinite article is used when saying what people's jobs are.)

4 Jack broke **his** leg skiing. (A possessive adjective is usually used before parts of the body.)

5 He's only 18 but he already has **his** own business. (A possessive adjective is usually used before *own*.)

6 I was on a business trip to **the** People's Republic of China. (*The* is not used with most countries but it is used for countries or places containing a common noun like *Republic*, *Federation* or *Kingdom*.)

7 Since they built the tunnel, fewer people are using **the** ferry. (*The* is often used with means of transport to refer to the type of transport being used, rather than a specific bus, car or boat, e.g. *I take the bus to work.*)

Extension activity

Ask students to prepare their own examples to illustrate each of the rules worked on in the Corpus spot.

Listening

1 Students should look at the pictures and speculate about the kinds of films or shows they might be from. Personalise the topic by asking students to talk about their own preferences.

2 **2 08** Play the recording once and ask students to think about questions a–c.

Suggested answers

a Two films: *The Stalker* and *Shakespeare in Love*.

b *The Stalker* by Russian director Andrey Tarkovsky, is hard to follow, has an interesting use of camera, music and dialogue.
Shakespeare in Love is based on the life of Shakespeare and suggests how he used his own love for Viola in his play *Romeo and Juliet*. We can't be sure how much it reflects reality.

c *amazing; didn't really understand what was going on; something incredibly beautiful and mysterious about it; stunning camera shot; evocative use of music; thought-provoking piece of dialogue; that's what I like about it; prefer films where I can follow the plot; really loved; gave me an insight; made me look at* Romeo and Juliet *in a new light; enjoyed it; totally convincing*

Recording script

Man: What would you say is your favourite film ever?

Woman: Oh. I can't stand that kind of question. I can never think of anything off the cuff. I've enjoyed lots of different films but I'd have to give it a lot more thought before singling out one. So, what's yours then?

Man: Well, I just loved *The Stalker*. You know, that amazing film by the Russian director Andrey Tarkovsky.

Woman: Oh, yes, I remember seeing that once. I didn't really understand what was going on, though.

Man: I don't know that I do even though I've seen it loads of times - but there's just something incredibly beautiful and mysterious about it. Each time I watch it, I notice something I haven't paid any attention to before – whether it's a stunning camera shot, an evocative use of music or a thought-provoking piece of dialogue – and I think that's what I like about it.

Woman: Well, I think I prefer films where I can follow the plot. I'm obviously much more low-brow than you. I really loved *Shakespeare in Love*, for example. I felt it really gave me an insight into life at that time and it made me look at the play *Romeo and Juliet* in a fresh light. The film shows how Shakespeare used that play as a vehicle for expressing his own real-life passion for Viola.

> **Man:** Yes, I enjoyed it too. But no one knows if there's any truth in it, do they? We don't know enough about Shakespeare's own private life.
>
> **Woman:** Maybe. But I found it totally convincing. I believe it's true. Even if that might just be wishful thinking!

3   Point out that these collocations all come from the texts they have read or listened to in this unit. Ask students to match the collocations in this exercise.

Answers

a	6, 10 or 11	g	3
b	12	h	5
c	1	i	4
d	6, 7 or 10	j	8 or 12
e	6	k	4 or 10
f	2	l	9

4   This exercise could be set for homework as revision of the collocations worked with in exercise 3.

Answers

a	Film buffs	e	crystal clear
b	gave; an insight	f	feelings; experienced
c	pay attention	g	ring true
d	wishful thinking		

5   Students should try to do this exercise before using an English–English dictionary to check their answers.

Answers

a	the phone	d	the ironing
b	a wish	e	your duty
c	time	f	an idea

6   Allow students time to think about what to choose and how to describe it. They should then explain their choices to their partner.

Extension activity

Students could get into groups, with each group focusing on one of the categories that the students are interested in. For example, you might be able to have a restaurant group, a website group and a film group. Allow students to join the groups dealing with the topics that they are most interested in. Within these groups, students choose one thing that they would definitely recommend and one that they would definitely not recommend. They list as many reasons as possible for their selections. When they are ready they present their recommendations to the rest of the class.

Writing folder 7

Student's book pages 110–111

Reviews

1 Discuss this question with the whole class. There are no right or wrong answers here, as the purpose of a review may well vary with its context, the writer's role, etc.

2 Establish if any students have seen the film being reviewed and if so, what they thought of it. Ask them to read the review and complete the lists. As a follow-up, ask students who have seen the film if they think the review is fair. Ask students who have not seen it to say if they would now like to.

> **Suggested answers**
> **Facts about the film and its plot**
> The name of the film is *Avatar*. It was directed by James Cameron. It used new 3D technology. The story is set a hundred years in the future.
>
> Actor Stephen Lang plays the role of Colonel Miles Quaritch, Sigourney Weaver plays the part of Dr Grace Augustine and Sam Worthington plays pilot Jake Sully.
>
> **Phrases that convey the writer's opinion of the film**
> among the greats; super-sleek 3D; eminently watchable and hugely entertaining sci-fi spectacular; unable to decide if ...; The digitally created world meshes pretty much seamlessly with ...; undoubtedly impressive; The effects of *Avatar* are certainly something to see ... But it's difficult to tell if cinema as a genre has really been changed or not; a truly fascinating story; What a great idea it is – and that is what makes it an experience.
>
> **Things included to interest and entertain the reader**
> the inclusion of super-sleek new-tech 3D; the 'quirky-scary CGI animals'; the planet's aboriginal inhabitants ... hugely tall blue quasi-humanoids called the Na'vi, who have pointy ears, flat noses, ethnic dreadlocks and beads; the exotic, subtitled language of the Na'vi; the love story; the battle scenes

3 The language of the review reflects and underlines the setting of the film. For example, adjectives like *quirky*, *scary* and *exotic*.

4 Encourage students to find examples of collocations and fixed phrases themselves in the review before they go on to do Exercise 5.

> **Answers**
> a flying
> b eminently
> c spiritual
> d fall
> e seamlessly
> f undeniably
> g mind-blowing
> h truly

5 This task helps students realise what features a review usually contains. All the points are important, depending on the focus of a review, and students should discuss why they are important.

6 Point out that this task takes the form of the tasks used in the Writing test (Paper 2). Emphasise that all four bullet points must be addressed in some way or the answer will not pass.

18 May I introduce ... ?

GENRE: Small talk
TOPIC: White lies

Speaking	Telling lies
Reading	Lying
Vocabulary	Collocations and longer chunks of language
Grammar	Emphasis
Listening	Small talk
Speaking	The truth game
Workbook contents	
Listening	Discussing a picture
Grammar	Emphasising (cleft sentences)
Reading	Matching paragraph headings
Vocabulary	Language chunks

Student's book pages 112–115

Lesson planning
SV   Any of the Vocabulary section could be set for homework.
LV   See the extension activities in the Grammar and Listening sections.

Speaking

1   Identify the jobs represented in the photos with the class as a whole. Students should then discuss the questions with a partner.

Reading

1   This article has been labelled as a C2-level text. It features a lot of language used in a playful, allusive manner. Focus students' attention on reading for gist as they read the text for the first time.

Suggested answers
a   He is at a party.
b   He is telling a lot of lies, pretending that he hears people, pretending that he knows people and so on.
c   Perhaps because he wants to make the other person feel good or because he wants to make himself look good.

2   Students should read the text again quickly if necessary, listing points as they read.

Answers
He mentions lying about b, c and f. With g, he pretends to like a joke that he didn't hear rather than pretending to like a joke that he didn't find amusing – students may or may not consider this last point a lie in that he only smiles rather than say anything.

3

Answer
no

4

Answer
He comes to the conclusion that it is sometimes a good idea not to be too honest. The reason is that being pointlessly honest can lead to long, tedious conversations which can even be embarrassing.

5

Answers
These words sound like other words:
kind has several meanings – the speaker uses it with the meaning of 'nice' in the phrase 'not at all kind' whereas the writer hears it with the meaning of 'sort' in the phrase 'the tall kind'.
panned it sounds similar to *bandit*
reign sounds like (is a homophone of) *rain*

6

Answers
1 c   2 b   3 a

7   Ask students to discuss this in pairs, to round off the section.

Vocabulary

1   This section has also been labelled as containing C2-level language, picking up from the article. Students look through the words individually and then check answers with the class as a whole.

> **Answers**
> a plainly   f sustain
> b caught   g counterfeit
> c exceptions   h panned
> d unconditional   i cryptic
> e common

2   Students do this individually, seeing who can complete the collocations first.

> **Answers**
> a 2   b 5   c 4   d 6   e 1   f 3

3   Students complete the sentences.

> **Answers**
> a common   e exception
> b catch   f great admirer
> c particularly   g field
> d tip of my tongue

Emphasis

The language here is covered on page 173 of the Grammar folder.

1   Discuss with the class as a whole. Elicit the point that sentence a is extended in sentences b and c. Sentence b emphasised that 'I must not do something'. Sentence c emphasises 'telling lies'. The focus of the message is at the start of each sentence.

> **E**xtension activity
>
> Look through a magazine or a novel or some other example of written English. See whether you can find any examples of cleft sentences.

2   Students form these sentences with a partner. Discuss their suggestions with the class as a whole.

> **Possible answers**
> a The girl / person (who) Paolo loves is Maria.
> b What happened was that Katya had an accident. / It was Katya that had an accident.
> c What Rolf won / The amount that Rolf won was a million dollars.

3   **2 09** This exercise makes students aware of other ways of emphasising.

> **Answers**
> 1 I do believe what you're saying. (auxiliary verb *do* added)
> 2 He's such a nice man and he's been so kind to us. (use of *so* and *such*)
> 3 Can you open the window? I'm boiling! (use of exaggerated lexis)
> 4 He's intensely jealous of his sister. (use of intensifying adverb *intensely*)
> 5 That joke is as old as the hills! (use of simile)
> 6 Little did he imagine what was going to happen next. (use of inversion after a restricting adverbial)
> 7 Never was so much owed by so many to so few! (use of inversion after a negative adverbial)
> 8 What on Earth is that man doing? (use of *on Earth*, only used after a question word)
> 9 I really like this exercise! (use of intensifying adverbials such as *really*, etc.)

4   Note that this kind of emphasis is often used when correcting a statement that someone else has just made. Practise saying the sentences with the class as a whole with a strong stress on the auxiliary verb.

> **Suggested answers**
> a Jake **does** admire her work.
> b I **do** love you.
> c Mary **did** do her very best.
> d I **did** use to be able to dive quite well.
> e They **have** agreed to help us.

5   Students work with a partner and prepare two-line dialogues. They then read them out to the class, making the stressed auxiliary verb more emphatic.

6   Ask students to write an appropriate response using a stressed auxiliary verb.

> **Answers**
> a No, I **am** right.
> b I **did** give you the right information.
> c I **do** help you with the housework.
> d He **didn't** cheat.
> e I **shall/will** be able to!
> f I **haven't** forgotten it!
> g Yes, she **is** going this year.

Listening

1 **2 10** Explain that students will listen to some questions similar to those they might be asked in the Speaking test (Paper 5). Play the first part of the recording and ask students to write down the questions they hear.

Recording script

1 Have you been enjoying your studies?
2 What interesting things have you done recently?
3 How would you feel about living abroad permanently?
4 How about your social life?
5 What are your plans for the future?
6 Have you always lived in the same place?
7 What would you say has been the most memorable event here so far?
8 Have you made any good friends here?

---

2 **2 11** Now play the full conversation. Students should listen and complete the table. When checking the answers, ask students what makes the better answer (it's either fuller or it answers the question that was asked).

Answers
Better answers are given by:
1 Yolanda
2 Martin
3 Yolanda
4 Martin
5 Martin
6 Yolanda
7 Martin
8 Yolanda

---

3 Play the full conversation again and ask students to note the main points made by the speaker who gives the better answer. These points are underlined in the script.

Recording script

Chris: So how are things with you both? Have you been enjoying your studies?

Martin: Well, actually I'm finding it quite hard. I think first of all the pronunciation of many words is very very different in English, something to do with the spelling maybe. There are very many words, so it's difficult to learn them all and the main thing I think is the verbs, I'm used to putting those at the end of a sentence, not at the beginning or the middle, so that's difficult.

Yolanda: I'm really enjoying it, now that I can speak English so much better, going to see films and understanding exactly what is going on. I also like listening to songs and knowing what they mean.

Chris: What interesting things have you done recently?

Martin: Well, funnily enough last Saturday I went to a football match, which I've never been to before, and that was a great experience, very exciting and it's good to be among so many people. I enjoyed that very very much.

Yolanda: I went to the supermarket. I took a bus around town, I visited some friends and I've also been reading a lot. Not so interesting, actually!

Chris: How would you feel about living abroad permanently?

Martin: Oh, that's something I would really like to do. I think you get a very interesting sense of yourself when you live abroad and you can meet very interesting people.

Yolanda: I have a friend who, a school friend, who went to live in France for a few months and he said that for the first two months it was very good, very exciting but after that he said that he started to miss his friends and his family, and he wanted to get home and it wasn't so good after that.

Chris: OK, and how about your social life? How are things in that respect?

Yolanda: Well, I don't really enjoy going to parties at all. I haven't got time.

Martin: For me it depends what kind of mood I'm in. Often I like going to parties where you can dance a lot and there's loud music playing and other times I like going to parties where you can talk to people and get to know them, get to meet them and I think most of all I like going to parties that last a long time, you know? They go on all over the weekend maybe, or – not just one evening.

Chris: And when you finish your studies? What are your plans for the future?

Martin: Well, my course lasts another three and a half months and as soon as that finishes, I'd like to do some travelling, around South-east Asia, if

I can, because that's a part of the world I'm really interested in, and then after another four months I am going <u>back home to see my family</u> and <u>go back to my studies</u> there.

Yolanda: Well, I don't know really. I haven't made any definite plans at the moment.

Chris: Have you always lived in the same place?

Martin: I've lived in a lot of different places.

Yolanda: Yes, I've <u>always lived in just one place</u> and for me I really enjoy this. It's a <u>great sense of community life</u> and I've known people in my village who have <u>known me all my life</u> and <u>I've known them for as long as I can remember</u>. <u>Whenever I go out, I meet someone that I know</u>. For example, all my friends from school still live in the same village and I, it's something I really really like.

Chris: What would you say has been the most memorable event here so far?

Martin: Er, I think probably last year, I was given my <u>birthday present</u> which was a <u>weekend course</u> in how to, <u>how to jump with a parachute</u>. And a few weeks later I went up in a plane and <u>I actually jumped out of the plane</u> with the parachute, and that was something I will remember forever, for sure.

Chris: Have you made any good friends here?

Yolanda: Yes, but I've kept in touch with my best friend. We talk nearly every day. Her name's Marisol and <u>she has a brilliant sense of humour</u>. She is also a <u>very good gymnast</u>. She is <u>18</u> years old and she has <u>short brown hair</u> and I have <u>known her since we were very young</u> and she is <u>very intelligent</u> as well.

Martin: Yes, Gerhard. I've known him since I started here, and he's, he's good, you know.

4 Ask students to look back at the nine questions they wrote down in exercise 1. They should ask each other these questions bearing in mind the advice they have read.

5 Refer students back to the reading text as they discuss this question. Encourage them to list things that they avoid talking about, as well.

6 **2 12** Play the recording when students have read through questions 1 and 2.

Answers
1 B   2 A

Recording script

Piotr: Oh, Jason, can I introduce Sophie? This is Sophie, she works in our Cologne office. Sophie, this is Jason.

Sophie: Hi, Jason.

Piotr: Jason's the manager of our branch in New York.

Sophie: Yeah, pleased to meet you.

Jason: And you. You're in Cologne, right?

Sophie: Yeah, that's right, yeah.

Jason: Yeah, did we meet before because I was in Cologne a couple of years ago? I don't think we met then, did we?

Sophie: No, I don't think so. I can't remember your face but I've only worked for the company for a couple of months you see, so ...

Jason: Oh, right, OK, so who did you work for before?

Sophie: Oh, well I was with Smith & Goldberg in Philadelphia.

Jason: Oh, really, in Philly? Excellent! I know it well, I grew up there, actually.

Sophie: Oh, really?

Piotr: I spent a year at graduate school there. Great place, isn't it, great place?

Jason: Yeah, yeah, great.

Sophie: Absolutely yeah, oh I loved my time there. I'd have been really happy to stay actually but ...

Piotr: Did you have to come back?

Sophie: Yeah, well, the thing is my husband's German so ...

Jason: Oh, right.

Sophie: Yeah, we wanted to come home and then we'd be closer to the family because when our little boy was born, we thought it would be nice for him, you know.

Piotr: How many children have you got?

Sophie: Well, now we've got a little boy, Adam, and we've got a girl as well called Maisie. Little girl, yeah, she's just two.

Piotr: Have you got children, Jason? I can't remember.

Jason: No, no, I don't have any kids right now but you know – never too late! So you know, of course I have to get a wife first but – you know, that could be arranged, I guess!

7 Play the recording again and ask students to take notes as they listen.

Answers
Jason: spent year at graduate school in Philadelphia, manager of branch in New York, was in Cologne a couple of years ago, grew up in Philadelphia, unmarried, no children
Sophie: works in Cologne office, has only worked for company for a couple of months, worked previously for Smith and Goldberg in Philadelphia, loved Philadelphia, husband is German, wanted to be closer to home when first child, son called Adam, was born. Also has little girl called Maisie.

ⓔxtension activity

Divide students into groups of three. They should role-play the situation they have just heard. They do not need to use the exact words from the recording but should act out a similar situation. They should then continue the conversation in any way that seems appropriate. Groups then compare the different ways in which they completed the situation.

Speaking

1 Point out to students that they may either tell the truth or invent a story (but if they invent something they should make it sound convincing). Ask them to work with a partner.

2 Students now work alone to think of two more questions for their partner.

3 As they listen to each other's answers, students note down whether they think their partner is telling the truth or not.

4 After they have asked each other all the questions, students should check whether they guessed correctly or not.

Exam folder 8

Student's book pages 116–117

Paper 1 Parts 1, 3 and 4 Multiple choice and multiple matching

Go carefully through both information boxes in this folder and point out that they are based on examiners' reports and on what candidates lose marks for in the exam.

1 Refer students to the Exam information box and ask them to bear in mind the points raised as they answer the questions.

Answers
1 B   2 C

2 Remind students to follow the points raised in the Exam information box as they answer these questions.

Answers
1 A   2 C   3 B   4 C, E   5 D   6 A   7 E   8 C
9 B, E   10 B

ⓔxtension activity

Each student thinks of two more questions. Their questions may relate to any of the films mentioned. They then give their questions to other students who have to answer the questions as quickly as possible.

19 Do it for my sake

GENRE: Proposals
TOPIC: Persuasion

Reading	Preparing a proposal
Grammar	Language of persuasion
Speaking	The perfect holiday
Vocabulary	Multiple meanings

Workbook contents

Use of English	Part 2 – open gap fill
	Part 4 – multiple meanings
	Part 5 – keyword transformations
Grammar	Language of persuasion

Student's book pages 118–121

Lesson planning

SV Grammar exercises 1 and 2 and Vocabulary exercises 1 and 2 could be set for homework.

LV See the extension activity in the Vocabulary section.

Point out to students that the language in this unit is useful for the exam because it deals not only with proposals and persuasion, but also with some of the most important exam topics (i.e. work, study and travel). Although these themes are dealt with elsewhere in the book, they are reviewed here as they are such frequent themes in the exam and are also topics that candidates are likely to find useful in 'real life'.

Reading

1 Ask students to read the adverts and decide who might apply for each one. In general, there are no right or wrong answers.

2 This question helps to personalise the situation.

3 First make sure that students understand what a personal statement is. Point out that they would need to write one if they were applying to study in a British university. Then discuss the task with the class. The point of this task is to raise students' interest in the kinds of issues that are dealt with in the reading text.

4 Students read the article on page 119 alone and do the task before checking answers with the class as a whole.

Answers

1 c   2 d   3 a   4 h   5 g   6 b   7 e   8 f

5 Students prepare their personal statements at home. Do this activity in a follow-up lesson. Ask students to scan the article again before reading their partner's statement. This may help to remind them of points that they may wish to comment on in the statement they read. It will also help to revise the language of the text.

Language of persuasion

The language here is covered on page 173 of the Grammar folder.

1 Refer students to the Exam spot at this point. Students then discuss questions a–d with a partner.

2 **2 13** Play the recording once and ask students to complete as much of the table as they can. Then they should compare their answers with a partner.

Answers

1	mother wants toddler to eat his vegetables	encourages, plays games, eats some too, praises
2	employee would like to take some time off work	reassures the employer that everything will be on track before leaving, and that they will always be contactable
3	boss wants workers to do some overtime	explains why it's necessary, shows sympathy with how workers must be feeling
4	girl wants friend to lend her a special dress to wear to a party	explains why she wants it so much, praises the dress, promises to do various favours in return, promises to be careful
5	sales person is trying to sell a fitted kitchen	uses very positive language about the offer, emphasises what a bargain it is, says it will all be very easy
6	teenager wants to persuade mother to let her stay out	reminds mum that there is no school next day, uses moral blackmail, tries to reassure mum, says all friends are going to be allowed, reminds mum how good she's been
7	wife wants to persuade husband that they should move house	emphasises benefits to children, says husband could use commuting time productively and so would be freer when home
8	sales assistant wants to persuade woman to buy dress	flatters, goes into detail about why the dress is good, points out how versatile it is

Recording script

Speaker 1: Now look, fish fingers and peas and carrots and broccoli. Oh, you like broccoli, don't you? Let me just put that on the fork. There, you have that. Go on, open your mouth. That's a good boy. You chew, that's it. And now a carrot. There you go, in it goes. You take that carrot, that's a good boy. Can I have some, can mummy have some? Oh, that's lovely, thank you. Now you have some, go on. You have that spoon. One for you, one for me. Good boy.

Speaker 2: Excuse me, have you got a moment? I wanted to ask you something, if I'm not disturbing you. The thing is, I'm owed a couple of days' holiday and I'd like to use them before the end of the year if possible. I appreciate it's quite a busy time for the department, but I'd really like to take next Thursday and Friday off. My brother's here and I'd like to spend a bit of time with him. We hardly ever manage to meet. Anyway, I'll make sure everything's on track before I leave, and I'll brief the PA so that she can deal with anything. But I don't expect there to be any problems. And you can always contact me, I'll have my phone with me.

Speaker 3: Now, I think you all know why we've had to meet today. I've got the monthly figures back from head office and for the third month running, sales are down and, well, we all know that things are getting tighter. It looks like I'll have to ask you to put in a little bit more overtime. No, no, I know, I know that's not going to be very popular but this is a good chance to make a bit more money. OK? I mean, this is probably just a temporary measure, but thanks for your understanding and all your hard work. Really appreciate it.

Speaker 4: Sorry, no. I don't want that, I don't want the red one. I actually just want to borrow the blue one. I wouldn't ask unless it was for this party. I mean, I've been, I just think he's going to be there and I'd just like to look nice and that dress is the most beautiful thing I've ever seen. Look, I won't spill anything on it, I promise, I won't even drink anything all night. I won't eat anything either. There'll be no crumbs, nothing, I promise. Look, I'll wash up for a month. I'll do all your washing. Oh, please let me?

Speaker 5: Good morning, I wonder if I could just take a few seconds of your time just to tell you about a special offer we're doing at the moment. We're in your area and we're doing free quotations on brand new kitchen units. Now these units are made to measure, they're marvellous, they're handmade by our craftsmen. Therefore it's very much cheaper buying them directly from our workshop than going to the shops and also you don't have to pay at all for anything this year, so basically we'll install the kitchen for you and you don't have to pay anything till next year. Now that's a fantastic offer, I'm sure you'll agree.

Speaker 6: All the others are going to be there and there's no school the next day. Do you remember you said that if I started doing better in maths you'd let me stay out? Well, I got good marks, didn't I? And I'll get a taxi home and I'll pay for it, so I'm not asking you to pick me up. Just this time. It's important. Everyone is going to be there.

Speaker 7: The thing is, I know it would be a bit more expensive to live there, and it's further away from work, but it's – I mean, there are so many good sides to it. We'd be closer to my mother, so she could help more looking after the kids. It's greener, everything's less stressful. You could go into work by train. You could work on the train – that'd be OK, wouldn't it? You like trains. That'd mean you could spend more time with the kids in the evening. What do you think?

Speaker 8: Yeah, the mirror's right over here, yeah. Oh, it really looks lovely. Yeah, oh, it's gorgeous on you though, you've got such a lovely figure. What size is that one? Oh, it's a size ten, yeah well there you are, you see. I can only get into size 12. You are lucky. Well, I'll tell you what, though. That dress really looks nice because the way it's cut over your hips, you see if you just turn round there, look, look in the mirror. It's ever so nice. And the colour's good on you as well because, like, green, green really goes with red hair. Yeah, oh, I think it's really nice. It's quite good because you can use that dress for all sorts of things, couldn't you? You could go to parties in it and wear it out anywhere, really.

3 Students discuss in pairs and then feed back to the rest of the class. The following are the sorts of points that should emerge.

Suggested answers

a This is a question. It is a hypothetical question in that it is assuming the 'yes'. It uses a conditional form of the verb and uses a relative clause to front the sentence (a cleft sentence). The adverb *surely* is used to emphasise the strength of the speaker's opinion.

b This is a sentence containing an adverbial clause of reason. It uses a conditional form of the verb and uses a relative clause to front the sentence (a cleft sentence).

c This is a short, simple question. *Why don't you* is used to make the sentence softer than an imperative.

d This is a sentence explaining what someone thinks. The word *that* could have been used after *think*. The adverb *really* and the modal verb *should* are used to emphasise the strength of the speaker's opinion and makes the sentence less formal than an imperative (e.g. *Try to save money this year.*).

4 Discuss with the class as a whole.

Answers
1 b   **2** a   **3** c and d

5 Students discuss which would be the better alternative with a partner before comparing answers with those of the rest of the class. As the answers are checked, discuss the register issues that are illustrated (e.g. how you persuade depends on the relationship between the speakers and the nature of the situation).

Answers
1 b   **2** a   **3** a   **4** a   **5** b

6 Point out that sentences 1, 3 and 5 are more formal.

Suggested answers
1 Have you got time to check through this report?
2 I'd rather you were more flexible.
3 You can't lend me some money, can you?
4 I'm sure everything will be fine.
5 Do you want to come with me?

Speaking

1 Students should first decide what the people would discuss.

Monitor the dialogues, then ask some of the students to act out dialogues to the rest of the class. Encourage them to put as much feeling into their dialogue as possible, as intonation is also important when trying to persuade people to do things. After listening to each of the dialogues, students comment on how effective they were.

2 Repeat this process for the dialogue between a parent and a child.

Vocabulary

1 Go through the Vocabulary spot with students, then ask them to do the exercise individually.

Answers
a single   **d** set
b break   **e** top
c degree

2 Ask students to work in pairs to think of at least two collocations for each word. Encourage them to use an English–English dictionary if they wish. As a follow-up homework, students could be asked to write sentences illustrating some of the collocations they found.

Suggested answers
keep a promise, **keep** hold of
back a proposal, **back** a car
follow your dream, **follow** suit
meet your match, **meet** a deadline
mark my words, **mark** time

Extension activity

Students could work with a partner and make up at least three sets of sentences like those in Vocabulary exercise 1. They should then work with another pair, testing each other on their sets of sentences.

Writing folder 8

Student's book pages 122–123

Proposals

1   Students should discuss these questions with a partner. Ask for their feedback, making sure the points mentioned in the answers below are covered.

If your students have had little experience of report or proposal writing, it may be helpful if you are prepared to give them an example or two of such types of writing that you have had to do. You could show this to them when they discuss 1b.

Discuss the answers to 1d with the class before reading the information given in the list that follows.

> **Suggested answers**
> a **Types of proposals**
>   academic proposal, e.g. about research with a view to getting some money or a place at university
>   work proposal, e.g. with a view to introducing some innovation at the workplace
>   social proposal, e.g. a plan for change that aims to persuade readers of the desirability of such changes
>   media proposal, e.g. to a publisher about something that you would like to write
>   political proposal, e.g. to the public saying what your party plans to do
> b student's own answers
> c It will probably have some or all of the following: a factual title; a clear statement of aims at beginning; facts presented unambiguously; clearly drawn conclusions at the end; headings used frequently to help clarify

2   Before they choose a writing task, remind students of the work they did on reports in Unit 7 and of the importance of using headings to signpost their writing. Then ask each pair of students to choose a task. Try to ensure that the three tasks are fairly evenly distributed among the pairs.

3   Students should now discuss these questions, bearing in mind the specific task they have chosen.

4   Students discuss questions a–c, noting down their answers. They may like to compare their answers with other pairs working on the same task.

5   The underlined expressions are ones that students should find useful. They may wish to make use of other phrases too. How they adapt them will depend on the task they have chosen.

> 1 The aim of this proposal is to put forward a piece of academic research that I would like to undertake.
> 2 This proposal outlines the scope of the new course being recommended, explaining why it would be of benefit to students. It then concludes with some suggestions as to how the course could be implemented most effectively.
> 3 There are a number of reasons why I wish to put this proposal forward.
> 4 There are a number of overwhelming arguments in favour of extending the computer centre at the college, rather than the sports facilities.
> 5 Firstly, the proposed new college magazine would help to create a stronger feeling of community within the student body.
> 6 Secondly, the proposed extension to the college library would serve the additional useful purpose of attracting more students to apply for courses here.
> 7 Despite the fact that the suggested programme might be expensive, the additional cost could be justified in terms of the benefits that participants would receive.
> 8 There are a number of recommendations that I would like to make.
> 9 Taking all the evidence into account, I recommend that the English Club should make some radical changes to its current programme.
> 10 I would urge you to give these recommendations serious consideration.
> 11 Please do not hesitate to contact me if you would like me to expand on anything in this proposal.
> 12 Having outlined the proposal in general terms, I would now like to discuss three key issues in more detail.

6   Students work individually to write a first draft of their proposal. In stage b it is probably more appropriate for students to work with someone other than their original partner, if possible, as a fresh pair of eyes may be helpful.

It may be useful to allow students to go over the proposals that they wrote, with the following procedure in mind.

Students exchange their work with a different partner. They read each other's work thinking carefully about these questions:

- Is the information totally clear?
- Are the headings informative?
- Are the paragraphs well-organised?
- Does the language seem accurate?
- Is the language varied in terms of both structure and vocabulary?
- What do I particularly like about this piece of writing?
- What suggestions could I make about how it could perhaps be improved?
- Students share their ideas about each other's work.
- Students rewrite their work in the light of any helpful suggestions they have received from other students.

20 Feeding the mind

GENRE: Talks
TOPIC: Food, pictures and science

Speaking	Food, pictures and science
Reading	Eating out, freezing food, a famous painting
Vocabulary	Word formation
Grammar	Inversion
Listening	A good talk
Speaking	Describing pictures

Workbook contents

Lecture	A lecture
Vocabulary	Word formation
Grammar	Inversion
Writing	An article

Student's book pages 124–127

Lesson planning
SV   Reading exercise 4 and Grammar exercise 2 could be set for homework.
LV   See extension activities in the Reading and Vocabulary sections.

Speaking

1   Students work with a partner to discuss the questions about photos A–C.

Reading

1   Remind students that being able to talk about pictures is an important skill for the Speaking test (Paper 5). Students work with a partner to write a sentence summarising each text. They should then compare their answers with another pair and decide on what they think would be the best sentence.

Suggested answers
1   There is a strong correlation between people's social background and the extent to which they go to restaurants or entertain people other than family for dinner.
2   Although the idea of freezing food to preserve it had occurred to Francis Bacon in the 17th century, the process was only developed commercially in the 20th century when Clarence Birdseye was inspired by native practices of freezing food in northern Canada.

3   Gainsborough's picture, *The Painter's Daughters Chasing a Butterfly*, is not only a portrait but also says a great deal about the passing of time.

2   Students skim the three texts and answer the questions as quickly as they can.

Answers
a 1   b 3   c 2

3   This time, allow students as long as they need to read the texts and answer the questions.

Answers
a 1   b 3   c 2

4   Discuss these questions with the class as a whole.

Suggested answers
a   Younger, single, highly educated people who earn more money.
b   Again, younger, single, highly educated people who earn more money.
c   People of all social groups.
d   They were both interested in the idea of preserving food by freezing it.
e   Bacon died and was not able to carry his experiment through.
f   Because the process of freezing prevents food from going off and it can be done so quickly that ice crystals do not form and thus spoil the cellular structure of the foodstuff.
g   Margaret is younger than her sister and looks less thoughtful and more instinctive.
h   That life is short perhaps, and childhood quickly passes.
i   This will depend on personal opinion but there are both happy elements (carefree scene, father's pride in his daughters) and sad elements (the fragility of life, the rapid passing of happy moments) in the painting.

5   Discuss this question briefly with students. If at least one student expresses a preference for each of the different texts, ask them briefly to explain why they liked that text best.

Extension activity

Ask students to identify the sources of the three texts. You may give them these alternatives to choose from.
• a magazine supplement from a serious newspaper (3)
• a sociological research report (1)
• a lay person's history of scientific breakthroughs (2)

Vocabulary

1   Students should do the exercise without looking back at the text. They should then check their own answers from the text.

> **Answers**
> 1   noun (*Painter*)
> 2   noun (*depiction*)
> 3   noun (*sentimentality*)
> 4   noun (*childhood*)
> 5   noun (*precision*)
> 6   adjective (*attentive*)

2   Identify the parts of speech required with the class as a whole. Students then go back and complete the exercise with a partner, filling the gaps with an appropriate word formed from the word in brackets at the end of each sentence.

> **Answers**
> a   adverb (*scientifically*)
> b   noun (*breadth*)
> c   adjective (*inconclusive*)
> d   adjective (*leisurely*)
> e   verb (*clarify*)
> f   adjective (*unhygienic*)
> g   verb (*defrost*)

Extension activity

For further practice, ask students to fill the gaps in the following sentences with an appropriate word formed from the word in brackets.
a   Phrasal verbs are used _____ in spoken English. (EXTEND)
b   There isn't a lot of _____ at that holiday resort. (ENTERTAIN)
c   Unfortunately, buses here run _____ . (FREQUENT)
d   The weather there in winter is quite _____ . (CHILL)
e   He hasn't studied English for a long time so he's planning to do a _____ course before going to work in Australia. (FRESH)
f   Your description is very _____ . You must rewrite it. (PRECISE)

> **Answers**
> a   adverb (*extensively*)
> b   noun (*entertainment*)
> c   adverb (*infrequently*)
> d   adjective (*chilly*)
> e   adjective (*refresher*)
> f   adjective (*imprecise*)

Inversion

The language here is covered on page 174 of the Grammar folder.

1   Look at the cartoons and discuss the example sentences with students. Elicit the point that the verb is inverted when the sentence begins with a negative or restricting adverbial.

> **Possible answers**
> 1   I have never had such poor service in my life!
> 2   You should not add more than a pinch of salt to the mixture!

2   Work through the sentences with the class as a whole.

> **Suggested answers**
> a   Never in my whole life have I tasted anything so awful.
> b   Under no circumstances are credit cards accepted.
> c   Not until much later did we find out about his research.
> d   Only when we arrived back at the lab did we realise what had happened.
> e   Not only did we lose our passports but also all our money.
> f   Only after she died did I learn her secret.

3   This exercise provides further practice of inversion in a more personalised way.

Corpus spot

Go through the information in the Corpus spot. Focus students on the word order of the sentences. Allow them to compare answers with a partner before giving feedback.

> **Answers**
> a   I **could never have** imagined how many arrangements were necessary.
> b   **Not only was** the host family kind, **but it was** also helpful.

Listening

1 **2 14** Students listen to the recording in which two speakers describe their favourite pictures. As they listen, students should note the main points made by the speakers.

Recording script

Speaker 1: I think my favourite photograph is the one I've got on my kitchen wall at home. It's – you've probably seen it, it's quite a common one. It's, it's a black and white photograph taken from, I'm going to guess something like the 1930s, and it's a few workers in New York high up, building a skyscraper or something, and they're taking a lunch break and they're all sitting on, on a girder or whatever it is and they've got their packed lunches and they're way way up high, and when I first saw this picture I, I couldn't look at it originally because, well, I don't have a great head for heights and so it just made me feel a bit funny about the whole thing because you can see, in the background you can see Central Park and the rest of Manhattan. And it's quite eerie but it's also extraordinary that they don't have any kind of safety gear on, and if you look at the left of the picture, there's, there's two guys, one of them is offering the other one a light for his, for his cigarette and every time I look at it, I keep imagining he's going to pull his hand forward as the guy reaches to try and light his cigarette and fall off. Maybe that just says something about me. But it's just, it's just such an evocative picture. It just makes me think of what conditions must have been like, the work conditions and there's something quite romantic about it, I suppose. We live in a sort of sanitised age and that kind of thing wouldn't happen any more but it's just, it's just a wonderful picture and they all look tired but just so contented so high up above the ground. It's quite extraordinary.

Speaker 2: The picture that actually comes to mind is something that I bought about a year and a half ago from the market. It was just staring at me. You know when you're sort of looking around and every time you turn round you keep seeing this picture. Didn't really have any money on me, shouldn't have been spending but I just fell in love with it. It's a huge black and white print in charcoal on textured paper. It's very sort of – you want to sort of get hold of it. At the time I was going out with a Taurus, so it seemed very right to go and buy it. I've just got it over my desk and it just seems to watch me wherever I am in the room. It's got a beautiful thick black frame as well. It's huge but I absolutely love it. I just really like the, the naive quality of the picture. It's very sort of childlike the way it's been drawn. I met the artist – she'd only done a couple of them – it was nice to meet the person who'd actually drawn the picture. It's just very special to me. Some people love it, some people hate it but I'm really glad I made that impulse decision and bought it.

2 Students discuss the talks, which both convey the speakers' feelings in a very articulate way. They are not formal, prepared talks, but the listener gets a clear impression of each picture and why it is special.

3 Students choose one of the topics to talk about and prepare their talk, bearing in mind content, delivery and use of language. Students could then volunteer to give their talk to the rest of the students in the class.

Speaking

1 Divide students into groups of four, A, B, C and D. Two students will be Examiners and two will be Candidates. Ask Students A and B to read the instructions on page 160 at the back of the Student's Book and make sure that they are clear about what they have to do. Point out that in Part 3 there is a list of topics for Students C and D to discuss – this is a bit different from Part 3 of the Speaking test, where they will be prompted by a collection of pictures.

After the students have done one set of interviews, ask the student who just listened in the Examiner role to give feedback on how well he or she thought the Candidates performed.

Then give students as much feedback as possible on how they performed both as Examiners and as Candidates. Make specific suggestions as to how their performance could be improved.

2 Now regroup so that Candidates become Examiners and vice versa. Ask students to do the same tasks, but point out that they should now be able to do them better.

Student's book pages 128–129

Topic review

Ask students to work with a partner to discuss questions a–i. The aim of this exercise is to encourage students to recycle the vocabulary and structures they have covered in the preceding units in a personalised way.

Writing

1 Students do stage a, preparing their proposal in groups. You may wish to do b–e in a follow-up lesson.

Vocabulary

1

Answers

a	eye	e	brains
b	heart	f	head, heels
c	feet	g	hair
d	hand	h	fingers

Grammar

1 Students prepare this individually and then compare their answers with a partner.

Answers

1	not	7	only
2	what	8	most
3	one	9	was
4	to	10	at
5	the	11	long
6	(a)round	12	a

Reading

1 Where there is any disagreement or doubt as to what the correct answers are, spend some time looking at the clues that can lead students to select the correct paragraphs to fill the gaps.

Answers

1 B   2 G   3 A   4 E   5 F   6 D

GENRE: Travel articles
TOPIC: Beauty spots

Listening	A natural wonder
Reading	Travelling through Tibet
Vocabulary	Idioms
Grammar	Range of grammatical structures
Writing	Register

Workbook contents

Listening	The Seven Wonders of Nature
Grammar	Range of grammatical structures
Writing	Describing a holiday

Student's book pages 130–133

Lesson planning

SV   Reading exercises 3 and 4 and Vocabulary exercise 2 could be set for homework.

LV   See the extension activities in the Listening and Grammar sections.

Listening

1   Ask students to work with a partner to discuss what they can see in the photos.

2   Ask students to suggest what the seven natural (not man-made) wonders might be. The key below gives one popularly accepted list, compiled in the US.

> The Grand Canyon, Arizona, US
> The Northern Lights (Aurora Borealis)
> The Great Barrier Reef, Coral Sea, north-east Australia
> Mount Everest, Nepal and China
> Rio de Janeiro Harbour, Brazil
> Victoria Falls, Zambia and Zimbabwe
> Parícutin volcano, Mexico

3   **2 15** Students listen to the recording. They should explain how the photos relate to what they hear. The underlined parts of the script show the answers.

Recording script

Located on the <u>northern tip of Australia's East Coast,</u> the tropical city of <u>Cairns is internationally recognised as the gateway to the Great Barrier Reef</u>, one of the seven natural wonders of the world. The city is home to 100,000 people and also <u>boasts the fifth busiest international airport in Australia</u> with many carriers flying direct to Cairns from countries around the world. Cairns has many outdoor restaurants and cafés and great shopping, and also offers a complete range of accommodation options from budget right through to five-star. <u>Great Adventures Cruises have been running trips to the Great Barrier Reef</u> for more than 100 years and, as a result, are recognised as an industry leader. Great Adventures offer day cruises to <u>Green Island, a beautiful 6,000-year-old coral bay</u>. It is perfect for lazing on white sands, swimming, or snorkelling around the surrounding reef or relaxing around the luxurious day-visitor facilities – <u>all just 45 minutes' crossing from Cairns.</u> A full range of options on the island include introductory scuba diving, certified scuba diving and guided snorkel tours, as well as a crocodile farm, parasailing and private beach hire. For those wanting the ultimate reef adventure, cruise from Cairns to the luxury of Great Adventures' <u>multi-level pontoon on the Outer Reef</u>. The pontoon features undercover seating and tables where you can enjoy a sumptuous buffet lunch. There's also a sundeck, full bar facilities, an underwater observatory, a semi-submersible coral viewing tour and a swimming enclosure for children. You'll be able to snorkel or dive among the reef's spectacular coral gardens and diverse marine life. <u>A once-in-a-lifetime experience</u>!

4   Students listen again. With a partner, they should change any false statements into true ones.

Answers

a   false: it is the fifth busiest international airport in Australia
b   true
c   false: it is 6,000 years old
d   false: it takes 45 minutes by boat
e   false: it is not all under water
f   false: *a once-in-a-lifetime experience* means that it is a very special experience, not that you are only allowed to go there once

5 Students should brainstorm all the things that the destination offers, which are underlined in the recording script. They then decide which are the three most attractive.

Extension activity

Because of the importance of the kind of language in this text for the exam, you might also like to read the recording script with your students and discuss any other aspects of the language that interest them. Point out that, at 270 words, this article is only slightly longer than the text that they are expected to write in Paper 2. Ask students to write a similar article about a tourist area in their own country.

Reading

1 The extract is about Tibet but do not tell students this yet, if they do not guess from the photos.

2 Students read the extracts first and then make notes on the points given.

Suggested answers
means of travel: car (Landcruiser)
driver's aim: to keep the car off the ground as much as possible
how Tashi felt about the journey: he seemed to enjoy it
difficult aspects of the journey: very bumpy
good aspects of the journey: good visibility and not much other traffic
scenery: mountains and river
what could be seen on the river: coracles (small boats)

3 Students read the second extract and underline the relevant words and phrases as they do so.

Suggested answers
village lined with waving Tibetan children
single- and double-storey buildings with walled-in courtyards
foothills behind the buildings
solid buildings with walls made of stone up to waist height and mud bricks above
window ledges with marigolds on them
black and white buildings
flags (blue, white, red, green and yellow) on flat roofs standing out against the rich blue sky with pictures of jewelled dragon-horse on them
copse of trees (willows or poplars) but landscape otherwise treeless
each courtyard wall piled high with firewood

4 Ask students to read the questions first and try to predict the answers. They should then read the text and answer the questions.

Answers
1 C   2 D   3 D   4 A

Vocabulary

1 With a partner, students match the idioms with their explanations. They may use an English–English dictionary if necessary.

Answers
on the roof of the world = at a very high (or the highest) altitude
a 6   b 2   c 4   d 5   e 1   f 9   g 7   h 8
i 10   j 3

2 Ask students to complete the sentences, putting some of the idioms into context.

Answers
a off the beaten track   d black spot
b hit the road   e no room to swing a cat
c picture-postcard

3 Students should discuss not only which expressions they would be likely or unlikely to find in a tourist brochure, but also why this would be the case.

Answers
Likely: *picture-postcard, stone's throw from* (the beach usually), *home from home*.
    These emphasise the attractive aspects of places.
Unlikely: *black spot, tourist trap, no room to swing a cat*.
    These emphasise unattractive aspects of places.

Range of grammatical structures

The language here is covered on page 174 of the Grammar folder.

1 Go through the Exam spot, then refer students back to the first part of *Running a Hotel on the Roof of the World*. Ask them to work with a partner and underline the different tenses and grammatical structures.

Suggested answers
Dorje had; which involved keeping; called out; whenever we were; grinning; bracing; would hit; it was hardly surprising that; would have made; is not hindered by; which are; appear; was how hard he could keep his foot pressed down; weighed against; could lead to; setting out; saw me trying to look at them; he shouted; it seems that; to make; are stretched; sewn; made from; are sealed with

2   Ask students to read the whole text first. They should decide which type of word goes in each gap, then fill in the correct word in an appropriate form from the words in brackets.

Answers
1   told / had told
2   was going to happen / would happen
3   was cycling / had been cycling
4   arranged / had arranged
5   lay
6   needed
7   set
8   saw
9   was sitting
10 looking
11 turned
12 smiled
13 rendered
14 thinking
15 came

3   Ask students to write a paragraph either on their own or in pairs, incorporating a range of structures and a range of descriptive vocabulary. The sentences given are intended as a starting point.

4   Students exchange their paragraphs and highlight any interesting vocabulary and structures.

5   Encourage students to improve on the paragraphs either by adding more descriptive vocabulary or making the structures more varied.

Extension activity

Students could write a story based on their paragraphs for homework.

Writing

1   Students should identify which sentences are more formal and which are more informal. Refer them to the Exam spot at this point.

Answers
It's a great hotel with loads of character.
The bedrooms get a bit chilly at night and the uncarpeted corridors can be noisy but it's worth putting up with a few minor inconveniences as it has so much atmosphere in other ways.
The food is fantastic and you can stuff yourself at breakfast so you don't need to eat again till the evening.

2   Personalise this reading activity by asking students which of the two hotels they would prefer to stay in and why.

3   Ask students to read the website information and then write in a similar style about Dalhousie Farm.

Suggested answer
Dalhousie Farm, old-fashioned with home-like atmosphere. Facilities include a restaurant, bar and a horse-riding centre. Activies on offer include guided treks, tennis, shore walks, sea fishing and golf. A range of rooms – 32 guest rooms and 13 garden suites – overlook a large private garden.

4   This writing task provides an opportunity for students to write a letter in a formal style.

Exam folder 9

Student's book pages 134–135

Paper 4 The Listening test

1 Ask students to ask and answer the questions on page 161. This checks that they know what to expect in the Listening test (Paper 4).

Answers
a four
b twice
c sentence completion, multiple choice, multiple matching
d on the sheet
e one
f Spelling is expected to be correct.
g 40 minutes
h 20%

2 Students should read through the questions and try to predict any likely answers. Students then listen to the recording and choose their answers.

3 **2 16** Students check their answers with a partner, then listen again. Go through the Exam information box with students.

Answers
1 D   2 B   3 A   4 D   5 C   6 A

Recording script

Interviewer: With me in the studio today is Julia Crawley, who runs a management consultancy which deals with women in business. Now Julia, if the majority of companies were run by women, what difference do you think it would make? I mean, what did you bring to the company you started?

Julia: Many people had warned me of the difficulties of being a female manager – to begin with, getting people to take you seriously. Male friends of mine in similar management roles always seemed to be worried about how long a woman would stay with a company and whether family commitments would mean she was less loyal than a male manager. I remember when I started as a manager it was natural for me, and I think it is for most women, to want to work with others, to see what they could contribute, and I told them what I was bringing to the table.

Interviewer: Mm. It is important that everyone realises they are important in a company, that every individual is as important as any other, isn't it?

Julia: One of the first female management gurus, Jennifer Alderton, put forward as her 'articles of faith' respect for all staff. She introduced me to the concept of power with rather than power over. Usually when power is discussed, it's taken to mean having power over someone else, getting that person to do what you want him to do, either through actual physical means or through persuasion.

Interviewer: And what do you see as being some of the drawbacks of the traditional male-run business?

Julia: Well, we've had hundreds of years of command control, maybe more, and it kind of works, although days can be lost as disputes are debated and in the meantime, machines are standing idle. And it's a very uncomfortable sort of organisation to work in, isn't it? I think now that people want more from their job; they don't want to be treated as an easily replaceable machine.

Interviewer: Mm. What other concepts that you value might we find in a female-run business?

Julia: Well, it would seek out differences. Say you'd been doing a particular procedure the same way for years and then someone challenged that. By positively encouraging criticism, you'd open up far more creativity and as a result the company would go forward at a faster pace. It's usually the people who have hands-on experience of systems that can see shortcuts.

Interviewer: And at the same time recognising that it's crucial for people to have a balance between their work and home life.

Julia: Yes, this is an issue which has been widely discussed in many countries and there have been some high-profile men and women who have given up highly paid, highly-responsible jobs because of the demand it was making on their time to spend more quality time with friends and family. The fact that these people were in the public eye has moved the debate on no end. I think where we need to go with this now is helping other countries where it is less acceptable for people to say, 'It's 6 o'clock, so I'm off now' to realise that good workers are alert workers who've enjoyed their free time and have slept well.

Interviewer: Is this where you're going to channel your efforts from now on?

Julia: It's tempting, because I can see that with better communication skills the workplace can become a far more attractive place to spend time. However, I'm getting involved in a scheme which backs small businesses which are struggling to get off the ground due to lack of cash. There are some great ideas out there with a demand for the product; but for a small company they've already invested all they had in setting up and getting a working prototype. So that's what appeals to me at the moment.

Interviewer: Well, good luck with that, Julia, and thank you for talking to us today.

4   **2 17** This is an example of a sentence-completion task. In the Listening test, there are eight questions in Part 2. Play the recording once.

Answers

a rebellion
b (an) organic (product)
c roots/origins
d presidents
e the knees ripped

5   Students go through the Exam information box and check their answers with a partner. Stress the importance of checking that the completed sentence makes sense and that the grammar is correct. Remind students also to check their spelling.

2 17 Students listen again to check their answers.

Recording script

When youth culture emerged in the early 1950s, jeans were a powerful symbol – a symbol of rebellion. They were frowned upon by your parents if you wore them when you went out. That was considered inappropriate because they were seen as work clothes. But, jeans went on to be adopted by young people across the world.

They were saleable across international boundaries because of their fantastic qualities, just as a product in themselves. They are what I'd call an organic product – the more you wear them the better they get. And on top of all that, you have this, this idea of youthfulness.

Remember, you know, culture in the 1950s was all coming from the United States. Rock and roll started in America, that's where its roots were, that's where the roots of jeans are.

Some people wonder if jeans have had their day now. They're not special any more. Some people have suggested that young people are going off jeans because the establishment are wearing them – we've seen presidents wearing them. But it's how you wear them that matters. You can wear them in a very different way to somebody else. Certain brands have that ability, like the Mini car – it can be driven by pop stars or little old grannies. Certain brands go beyond something that's only worn by one group after a period of time and jeans are certainly like that. So now it's the brand you wear, how you wear them, do you wear them loose or tight, washed out, with a crease down them? The codes become smaller and smaller. And you can still rebel in jeans. If you went somewhere very smart and you wore jeans with the knees ripped, that would be a symbol of rebellion. And all this means jeans are here to stay.

6 **2 18** Go through the introduction on Part 4 of the Listening test (Paper 4). Ask students to listen to the recording and match the speakers (1–5) with their relationship to Sara (A–H).

Answers
1 D   2 B   3 C   4 G   5 H

7 **2 18** Students should listen again and match the speakers with their opinions of Sara. Remind them that in the exam, they will have to complete both tasks as they listen.

Answers
1 B   2 C   3 F   4 G   5 A

Recording script

Speaker 1: It's funny how we became friends, I mean that doesn't usually happen with clients, but Sara's so outgoing. We got on like a house on fire. We chatted away while I was trimming, colouring or whatever it was and then she started bringing her daughter in too and we'd put the world to rights as I cut. And then one day she said she was having a barbecue and would I like to come along. Not many who come to the salon would do that. And since then we've become good friends.

Speaker 2: At first I thought she was a bit bossy, but after a while I realised that it's just her way of getting things done with the minimum amount of fuss and I must say she's great to share an office with. We usually take our breaks together. Last year we started going to the gym together after work on Wednesdays. She as hardworking in the gym as she is in the office.

Speaker 3: She's been such a help. I mean, more and more we rely on parents getting involved and helping out with social events. Sara's a great organiser. I know if I hand over something to her, it'll be done immediately, before you've had time to blink. Her daughter's the same. We wanted to have a sports day to help raise money for some new equipment that we need for the music department. I just mentioned it to Sara and the next thing I knew, there was a list of activities and who would supervise them on my desk. I wish she worked with me full time!

Speaker 4: It seems like I've known her forever. She's really changed, though. You'd never believe it but she used to be quite shy. She'd never speak up in class unless directly asked. But she was always hard-working, always did her homework on time. In year eight she won a prize for creative writing. She had been quietly developing into a very clever young woman.

Speaker 5: We met while we were both on the exercise bike. I'd been going there for ages but straight away she made me see that I wasn't really working very hard. She's got so much energy. We did the half-marathon together last year. I wouldn't have done it alone without her. If she makes up her mind to do something, she'll do it. I suppose that's how she got where she is today.

22 Under the weather

Speaking	Discussing the climate
Reading	Global climate change
Vocabulary	Weather and climate
Grammar	Interpreting and comparing
Listening	Aspects of climate change
Vocabulary	Describing change

Workbook contents

Listening	Climate change
Vocabulary	Climate change
Grammar	Interpreting and comparing
Use of English	Part 4 – multiple meanings
	Part 5 – key word transformations

Student's book pages 136–139

Lesson planning

SV Vocabulary exercise 1 could be set for homework.
LV See extension activities in the Speaking, Vocabulary and Grammar sections.

Speaking

1 As a lead in, elicit from students the meaning of the unit title, *Under the weather* (feeling ill, or a little sad). Then introduce the topic of the weather by asking students which aspects of weather the photos illustrate. Allow students time to discuss questions a–e, then get some feedback from the group as a whole.

ⒺExtension activity

Ask students to work in small groups and brainstorm vocabulary for severe weather conditions / natural phenomena. Give an example to get them started, e.g. *hurricane*.

When they have finished, elicit the vocabulary from students and write it on the board.

Possible answers
drought, flood, frost, hail(stones), heatwave, hurricane, storm, thunder and lightning, tornado

For question d, elicit students' personal experience of severe weather conditions, if you think this would not be distressing.

Reading

1 The aim of these questions is to raise students' awareness of whether what they read is fact or opinion, or something between the two (an opinion based on fact and an educated guess). Ask students to read the article and answer the questions.

Answers
a A mixture – there are facts about what scientists have discovered and predictions about the future which are educated guesses.
b Three: the IPCC, Dr Wainwright and Mark Gibson.
c **IPCC:** debate about how high the rise in temperature will be; discovery that Earth is less able to absorb carbon dioxide; predictions about what a 4°C increase would mean
Dr Wainwright: feedbacks in global carbon cycle and what that means; humans to blame for increase in temperature
Mark Gibson: 4°C rise not inevitable; ways to mitigate predicted rise in temperature

2 This question deals with recognising how sure people are when they present facts and opinions. Ask students to work on the activity in pairs.

Answers

IPCC	*is more likely*	sure
	have discovered	sure
	it would wipe out	sure
	would be displaced	sure
	is likely	sure
Dr Wainwright	*have discovered*	sure
	seem to be adding	not so sure
	could mean	not so sure
	there is little room for doubt	sure

Vocabulary

1   This exercise could be set for homework.

Extension activity

Write these phrases on the board. They are all taken from the article.

their starkest warning yet
dire predictions
it would wipe out hundreds of species
the 2007 report painted a gloomier picture
there is little room for doubt

Ask students to look at the phrases in context in the article and deduce the meaning of the underlined words. Using an English–English dictionary, students could give some examples of the words in phrases or sentences. For example, *stark* can mean 'severe' as in *a stark warning*, or 'desolate' as in *a stark landscape*, or 'absolutely' as in *stark naked*.

2   This exercise practises collocations connected to the topic of weather.

Answers
a 5   b 6   c 4   d 1   e 2   f 3   g 9
h 7   i 8

3   Students now practise some of the collocations by putting them into context within the blog.

Answers
1   torrential rain   4   sea defences
2   ice cap   5   below freezing
3   high tide(s)

Interpreting and comparing

The language here is covered on page 174 of the Grammar folder.

1   Students discuss their answers in pairs before comparing them with the class.

Answers
1   main weather features   5   pollution
2   Rio de Janeiro   6   temperatures
3   Stockholm   7   humidity
4   visibility   8   Buenos Aires

2   Students match the features.

Answers
1 c   2 A   3 D   4 B

Extension activity

Get students to find out about weather in major cities they know and make a similar chart to the one provided. Alternatively, you could use the Internet to find information about the cities in the chart for the date when you are working on this unit.

Go through the information in exercise 1 and then refer students to the Exam spot. Explain that the examples provide phrases which students can adapt and use when talking about statistics.

Here are some further examples of general statements which give examples of different connecting phrases:

- *Britain has a temperate climate.* **By way of contrast**, *Hong Kong has a tropical climate.*
- **In comparison with** *Mexico, Sweden experiences colder temperatures.*
- **Many people believe that** *the whole of the African continent is hot and dry.* **On the contrary**, *there is a huge variety of climatic conditions throughout the continent.*
- **Although** *some areas of Australia are desert, many others produce lush tropical jungle.*
- **While** *Siberia experiences some of the coldest temperatures imaginable, other parts of Russia enjoy a subtropical climate.*
- *The west of Britain has quite heavy rainfall* **whereas** *the east receives comparatively little rain.*

3   Students should read the whole text first, then complete the gaps with an appropriate linking device from the box.

Answers
1   On the other hand   4   contrary to
2   Indeed   5   However
3   whereas   6   because

4   If students find this exercise difficult, give them some help by providing the first, fifth, tenth and last word for each sentence.

Answers
a   In conclusion, we can say that the world's temperature has risen significantly over the last couple of decades.
b   On the whole it may be said that / It may be said that, on the whole, we are experiencing more extreme weather conditions.
c   Therefore, it can be concluded / It can therefore be concluded / It can be concluded, therefore, that scientists are following all climate changes with increased interest.
d   Given this, it may be deduced that unless countries reduce carbon emissions, the climate is under threat.

Listening

1 **2 19** Before playing the recording, check that students understand the vocabulary listed in the table.

> **Answers**
> **Peter**: floods, global warming, greenhouse gas emissions, sea level, storms
> **Anna**: El Niño, floods, droughts, global warming, storms

---

Recording script

Peter: Some people say, good, it's great if the world's warming up. We'll have better holidays. But if they stopped to think for a second, they'd realise it's serious. I mean, if it gets warmer, it stands to reason that more water will evaporate from the oceans and surely that means more storms somewhere else. There's evidence that there are more storms, hurricanes and so on and that they're more intense. Now that more accurate records are kept we can see that global warming is a fact.

Another aspect of global warming is how this will affect the sea level – it'll definitely rise. I read something recently which suggested that the sea might rise by as much as half a metre over this century, you know, because as the ice melts, the oceans expand. Imagine what effect that'll have on low-lying areas around the world.

Another thing that gets me is that we know all this and yet we're not reducing our greenhouse gas emissions anything like fast enough to stop the effects of climate change. We might be able to slow it down a bit but I think that's all.

Anna: I know it seems as if there are more cases of extreme weather, like floods and droughts, but I wonder if it's only that we hear about them more than before because of the news on TV and the fact that now it's easier to communicate world events to everyone and very quickly. Surely there's always been severe weather. Storms are a natural phenomenon, after all.

I admit there is evidence of global warming, but is there evidence to show that that's what's causing severe weather? Maybe we would have had these typhoons and floods anyway? I mean no one even really knows how storms form and the path they'll take. You see, what it is, is that the consequences are much greater these days. The world is more densely populated so in terms of the effect on population and financial loss the results are more devastating.

Everybody's heard of El Niño and La Niña, but from what I hear, we still don't know whether it's global warming that's making things worse.

---

2 Ask students to listen again and make more notes about the speakers' views.

3 Then ask students to work with a partner and compare and contrast the speakers' views, using linking devices, as appropriate.

Vocabulary

1 and 2 These words will be useful to students when interpreting information in charts, graphs or statistics.

> **Answers**
> 1 increase ↗
> 2 rise ↗
> 3 decrease ↘
> 4 decline ↘
> 5 reduction ↘
> 6 fall ↘
> 7 drop ↘

3

> **Answer**
> both (it describes an unstable condition)

4

> **Answers**
> a slight
> b gradual
> c significant, steep, sharp
> d rapid, sudden

5 Put students in pairs (A and B) and direct them to the right page in the back of the book. Students must not look at each other's charts. Ask students to work together to fill in the missing information in their diaries, using linking devices and vocabulary for describing trends as appropriate. They should make sure they follow the instructions given in the four bullet points very carefully after they have exchanged the missing information.

Writing folder 9

Persuasive writing

1   The aim here is to show that many types of writing requested in the Writing test (Paper 2) include an element of persuasion. Discuss the first one as a class and then students complete the exercise in pairs.

Possible answers

1   You will be trying to persuade readers of the college magazine of the importance of the issue of climate change. You want to persuade them because you feel passionately about the subject. Arguments you might use – everyone needs to play their part if the problem is to be solved, the problems will be far greater if we do not take action now.

2   You will be trying to persuade readers of the website of your opinion of the album. You want to persuade them because it is something that you feel strongly about – you want to share your enthusiasm, perhaps. Arguments you might use – the quality and originality of the music.

3   You will be trying to persuade the management of a tour company of the need to give your friend the job they have advertised. You want to persuade them of this because you want to help your friend. Arguments you might use – your friend is ideally suited for the job, he or she is totally trustworthy, gets on well with people and so on.

4   You will be trying to persuade fellow students of what you consider the best ways to prepare for exams. You want to persuade them of this because you want to help them do well. Arguments you might use – preparing effectively will mean less stress, better marks, etc.

5   You will be trying to persuade English-speaking visitors to your area that certain walks are worth doing. You want to persuade them of this because you want them to share places that you have enjoyed. Arguments you might use – they will find these walks beautiful, they will see things that many tourists never discover.

6   You will be trying to persuade your teacher to your point of view about the suitability of the set text for future classes. You want to persuade him or her of this because you either want or do not want other students to share your experiences of the text. Arguments you might use: it does (not) help with English studies; it is (not) enjoyable and interesting.

7   You will be trying to persuade the company that they should either give you your money back or a replacement gadget. You want to persuade them of this because of your disappointment that the gadget no longer works. Arguments you might use – the gadget does not do what it claims on the box or in the adverts, the company has a good reputation.

8   You will be trying to persuade the principal of the college to agree with your opinion about how the funding will be spent. You want to persuade him or her of this because you want yourself and/or other students to benefit from the funding. Arguments you might use – what you suggest will help students in their studies, it will enhance the college's reputation.

2   Discuss this with the class as a whole. Point out that each pair of sentences relates to the situation of the same number in exercise 1.

Answers

1   a is better as b is far too dismissive for a sensible argument on a serious topic.

2   b is better – it gives far more information and is more reasoned.

3   b is better as it is using more meaningful vocabulary. It also provides sounder reasons for offering Anna the job.

4   a is better as it makes a practical suggestion rather than being rude about people who do not take the approach recommended as rudeness is likely to antagonise readers.

5   a is better as it explains things using more interesting vocabulary and structures.

6   a is better because it is more polite and is offering a constructive suggestion rather than being negative.

7   a is better because it is polite while still being firm, while b is unnecessarily aggressive for an initial letter of complaint.

8   a is better as it sounds polite and gives a convincing reason for the opinion.

3   This task draws students' attention to the importance of planning a piece of writing. Accept any logical order suggested by students.

4   Steps a–e here will help students to identify the key parts of the question and to organise their ideas.

Suggested answers

a   contribution; college magazine; climate change; serious concern; measures students could take

c   fellow students

d   lively and entertaining

e   *climate change as serious issue*: effect on food production; effect on populations in different parts of the world; flooding; effects on wildlife; melting ice caps; more serious climate events (hurricanes, drought, etc.) *measures students can take*: recycle; reduce carbon footprint; walk or cycle rather than drive; take train rather than fly; use low-energy light bulbs; switch things off when not in use, etc.

5

> **Suggested answers**
> a **Introduction:** how climate appears to be changing
> **Second paragraph:** the impact that climate change may have on the world in general
> **Third paragraph:** the impact that climate change may have on the country where you are
> **Fourth paragraph:** what students can do to help combat the impact of climate change
> **Conclusion:** a final strongly worded encouragement for students to do as you recommend
> b There are no right and wrong answers here. It would be quite possible to use all these forms in answer to this task but which ones students select will depend on their own view of how they are going to do the task. The important point is that they should be aware of the need for variety in terms of structure as well as vocabulary.

6 Students write their first draft.

7 Explain how you would like students to edit each other's first drafts. Go through the correction codes and give an example of each one if necessary.

8 The final version could be set for homework if time is short.

23 I really must insist

GENRE: Formal letters
TOPIC: Putting your point across

Speaking	Personality quiz
Reading	How to complain
Grammar	Phrasal verbs (2)
Listening	How to ask for a pay rise
Writing	A letter of complaint
Speaking	Getting your views across

Workbook contents

Reading	Letter of complaint
Vocabulary	Collocations; formal phrases
Writing	A formal letter of apology
Grammar	Phrasal verbs (2)

Student's book pages 142–145

Lesson planning
SV   Grammar exercise 3 and Writing exercise 2 could be set for homework.

Speaking

1   Introduce the unit by asking what someone might be going to say if they start with the phrase *I really must insist*.

Explain that the situations in the quiz are ones in which people might feel they want to complain. Ask students to work with a partner and discuss what they would do.

When students have had enough time to talk about the situations, invite them to suggest alternative answers.

Students look at the key on page 162 and discuss whether or not they agree with the comments.

2   Ask students to discuss questions a–c to personalise the topic further.

Reading

1   Ask students not to look at the article while making their list of pieces of advice.

2   Students should read the article (this could be set for homework if time is short) and match the headings to the paragraphs. Then ask if the advice they listed in exercise 1 was in fact mentioned in the article.

Answers
1 D   2 H   3 F   4 A   5 G   6 C

Check that students have understood the vocabulary in the article, especially idioms such as *spouting hot air* (= saying a lot of things in a very angry way).

3   Encourage students to give their own views about the advice given in the article.

Phrasal verbs (2)

The language here is covered on page 175 of the Grammar folder.

1   Ask students to work in pairs and to answer the questions about the examples from the article.

Answers
gear up = get ready for. You can use an object but you need to add *for* (e.g. *gear up for battle*). This phrasal verb is inseparable.
find out = get to know/discover. You can use an object. This phrasal verb is separable.
go ahead = continue/do what you intend to do. You cannot use an object. This phrasal verb is inseparable.
carry out = do for real / execute. You can use an object. This phrasal verb is separable.

2   Go through the Corpus spot. Point out that it is a common mistake to use the wrong preposition. Ask students to correct the sentences if necessary. You could point out that five of the sentences are correct.

Answers
a ✓
b I **looked through the guarantee** but I couldn't find out how long it was valid for.
c ✓
d ✓
e We don't **hold out much hope**, but we are still trying to get compensation.
f Trying to get a satisfactory to my queries **took up** the whole morning.
g ✓
h ✓

3 This could be set for homework if time is short. It allows students to use some more phrasal verbs in context.

Answers

1	plucked up	5	to put across
2	get on with	6	sink in
3	make out	7	took to
4	stick up for	8	turned out / turns out

Listening

1 Ask students to discuss the pre-listening questions with a partner. These should get students thinking about the issue of asking a boss for a pay rise. Allow some time for class feedback.

2 **2 20** Give students time to read through the questions before playing the recording. Refer them to the Exam spot at this point.

Answers

1 C 2 B 3 A 4 A 5 B 6 C

Recording script

One of the most important situations in our professional life is when we feel we have to ask for a pay rise. It can be awkward but if you aren't assertive and you don't say what's on your mind, it may lead to you feeling undervalued and having a negative attitude to your work and workplace.

A positive attitude, forward planning and perfect timing are the keys to getting a pay rise. You may be asking for a number of reasons, ranging from a bigger workload or the increased cost of living to the fact that you've found out that a colleague is getting more than you. But these arguments will be secondary to your worth to the company.

Start by taking an objective look at your career. Are you good at your job? Are you punctual and reliable? Do people know who you are, and for the right reasons? Are you worth more than you're getting paid? If so, how much?

Are there any problems that you need to address? If so, make the changes subtly, over a period of time. Bosses are not stupid, and sudden bouts of punctuality just prior to a pay negotiation will seem like the worst type of creeping.

When planning your negotiation, don't base it on your gripes. Even if you think your future in the company doesn't look too rosy, bear in mind the 'what's in it for me?' factor. You may want extra money for all those things that are on your want list, for a holiday or a car, but your boss will be more convinced by an argument based on your quality of work and dedication.

To strengthen your viewpoint, plan for potential objections. If your boss is going to resist, what points is he or she likely to bring up? You could raise some first, along with arguments in your defence. For example, the sort of line you could take is, 'I know most pay rises are linked to set grades in this company, but I believe that my job has changed sufficiently to make this an exceptional case.'

Bartering can be embarrassing, but you will need to feel and sound confident. Remember that negotiations are a normal part of business life. Never pluck a sum out of the air. Know exactly what you will ask for and what you will settle for.

The timing of your communication can be crucial. Keep an eye on the finances and politics of the company to avoid any periods of lay offs or profit dips. If your boss can be moody, get an appointment for his or her most mellow time of the day. Never approach the subject casually. Being spontaneous might make your boss nervous.

There's always the chance that you won't get what you ask for. This is often the point at which reasonable demands and negotiations can turn into conflict. Never issue ultimatums, and don't say you'll resign if you don't mean it. Boost your confidence and your argument by having a backup plan (that is, what you'll do if you don't get the pay rise you want). Plan for the future by staying positive, asking when you could next apply and what can be done in the meantime to help your case.

Writing

1 Go through the Exam spot and ask students to bear this in mind when they write their letter. Then ask students to read the writing task and discuss questions a and b. Their answers will vary here.

2 If time is short, the letter could be set for homework. To mirror exam conditions, ask students to write approximately 220–260 words.

Speaking

1 Go through the bullet points with students and then ask them to tick the ideas they think are important and useful. Encourage them to give reasons. When they have finished, students should compare their suggestions with those of another student. Invite students to suggest more points to add to the list (e.g. using intonation for emphasis).

2 Go through the Exam spot. Point out that interactive communication is one of the criteria that examiners give marks for in the Speaking test.

Exam folder 10

Student's book pages 146–147

The Speaking test

1   This Exam folder provides practice in all four parts of the Speaking test (Paper 5). Go through the introduction with the students. Ask students to work in pairs and to discuss questions a and b. It's important for students to be able to discuss their feelings about the speaking test.

Answers
a   students' own answers
b   Examiners are looking for a range of accurate grammar and vocabulary, discourse management, clear pronunciation, and ability to display interactive communication. For further information about these assessment criteria go to www.cambridgeesol.org.

2   Ask students to work in pairs and to tick the points they mentioned in exercise 1 and to discuss the points they didn't mention. There are many different things that you can say about these images, of course. First, you could think about what each person is doing. In A, the person is rock-climbing; in B, decorating a new flat; C, taking a driving lesson. Think about why each person might be doing the activity, and how they are feeling. Make sure you answer the question by giving possible reasons as to why each person chose to do each activity.

3   This question gives practice of Part 1 of the test. Encourage students to expand their answers and to answer the question precisely. Monitor as they work and give constructive feedback.

4   This question gives practice of Part 2, when candidates are asked to comment on and/or react to a set of pictures.

5   Students work together on this task, which helps to prepare them for Part 3. Students don't have to agree with each other. Monitor to make sure students are making equal contributions. It's hard to imagine how a chess set would be of use in language learning as chess is largely played in silence. But, you should be able to think of ways in which all the other pictures illustrate something that would have a place in a self-access centre.

6   This question helps to prepare students for Part 4, in which students participate in a wider discussion of the issues raised in Part 3. Give feedback on the students' performance.

24 News and views

GENRE: Investigative journalism
TOPIC: Stories in the news

Speaking	Finding out about the news
Reading	A news article
Vocabulary	Choosing language
Listening	News broadcasts
Grammar	Connecting words

Workbook contents

Use of English	Part 2 – open gap fill
Listening	Citizen journalists
Vocabulary	Guessing meaning from context
Use of English	Part 3 – word formation
Grammar	Connecting words

Student's Book pages 148–151

Lesson planning
SV Vocabulary exercise 2 could be set for homework.
LV See the extension activities in the Vocabulary and Listening sections.

Speaking

1 Ask students to work with a partner to discuss questions a–c.

Reading

1 Students should discuss the pre-reading questions as a lead in.

2 Check that students understand the verb in the headline *to binge* (to eat in an uncontrolled way). Then ask them to read the article and choose the correct statements.

Answers
1 C
2 B
3 C

3 These questions allow students to react to the article in a personalised way. If students can't think of examples for question c, write some of the following on the board and ask the class to discuss their opinions: *cloning, designer babies, prolonged lifespans.*

Vocabulary

1 Discuss the point that journalistic language is often quite distinct. Journalists like to use interesting and dramatic language. Ask students to find the words individually.

Answers
a	found	e	identified
b	cascade	f	deactivate
c	craving	g	artificial
d	resist	h	expose

2 This exercise could be set as homework.

Answers
a	resist	d	artificial
b	deactivate	e	cascade
c	craving	f	expose

3 Ask students to do this without referring back to the article.

Answers
a 4   b 5   c 1   d 2   e 3

4 Remind students that they may need to change the form of the verb. This exercise could be set as homework and then checked in a follow-up lesson.

Answers
1 conducting an experiment
2 come to the conclusion
3 risking their health
4 raised the possibility
5 find it hard

Extension activity

Ask students to look for collocations in both the main article and its continuation in exercise 4.

Possible collocations
binge on chocolate; notice differences; contain information; initiate events; have a sweet tooth; provide with an excuse; express interest; boost immune systems

Listening

1   **2 21** Play the recording once and ask students to complete the summarising sentences individually. They should then compare their answers with a partner before listening again to check.

Recording script

I'd like to finish this week's edition of *News Weekly* by telling you a little about what's happening in next week's programme. Because of next week's sports events, *News Weekly* is being broadcast on Thursday rather than Tuesday. It will be shown at its usual time of half past eight. The programme's entitled 'The Golden Age' and it's an extended programme lasting an hour rather than the usual 40 minutes. The theme is contemporary youth. *News Weekly* is conducting an investigation into modern teenagers and their lifestyles. We usually record our programmes in London but next week, we'll be focusing on young people in rural parts of the country. There are plenty of programmes about young people in urban areas – this is something different and we're sure you'll find the results fascinating.

It touches on a number of issues – modern teenagers' attitudes to work, to friendship, to leisure, among other things. It looks most deeply at how young people feel about education and it comes up with some surprising conclusions. At the end of the programme there will be an opinion poll which we're hoping that all our viewers will take part in – you'll be able to call in on the usual number.

There is also a special website dedicated to this programme. This'll host a discussion after the programme has been broadcast, dealing with issues that it raises.

News Weekly is planning to investigate a number of other controversial issues over the coming months. It will, for example, dedicate a couple of programmes to the complex relationship between crime and poverty. ...

2   Students discuss the photo. Write their ideas on the board.

3   **2 22** Now play the news item and ask students to make notes.

Recording script

The night sky lit up last night in a glowing fireworks finale of a winter games that organisers say boosted the Paralympic Games to a new level worldwide.

Sir Philip Craven, President of the International Paralympic Committee, told the closing ceremony that these Winter Games had been 'the best ever'.

Amid a glittering display of skiers bearing torches down the mountain, dance and sports demonstrations, the official flag of the games was lowered to the sound of the Paralympic theme.

'Many of you will go home as champions, you all go home as winners,' John Furlong, CEO of the organising committee, told more than 500 athletes and hundreds more officials from 44 countries, as well as thousands of spectators before an outdoor stage.

'You have been remarkable ambassadors of the human spirit,' added Furlong.

Officials said these Paralympic Winter Games had drawn an international audience via national television broadcasts and internet viewers that set records for both winter and summer games, while a record 85 per cent of all tickets were sold for alpine skiing, biathalon and cross-country skiing, wheelchair curling and ice-sledge hockey events.

4   **2 22** Ask students in pairs to discuss whether they can answer any of the questions before listening to the recording for a second time.

Extension activity

Ask students to retell the two news items in their own words.

5 Elicit what the phrase *labour laws* might refer to and how these might be broken. Answers could include the minimum age at which children can start work, the legal maximum number of hours worked, safety and hygiene regulations and the minimum wage.

6 **2 23** Ask students to listen and answer questions a–e.

> **Answers**
> a no
> b employing children and not paying workers the minimum wage
> c Workers are working illegally and therefore don't want to complain or they are so desperate for the work that they think it's better to have any job rather than no job at all.
> d Her boss said he would report her to the authorities and say she had lied about her age.
> e no

Recording script

Working undercover, I have discovered that many companies throughout the world are flouting the child labour laws and minimum-wage laws. And you can't pin this down to one particular part of the world or say that it only happens in big cities as opposed to country areas. I have witnessed with my own eyes child labour with workers being paid well below the legal requirements in every type of work you can imagine, from agriculture to clothes factories. Unfortunately it's very difficult to get workers to complain and the reasons are numerous, from they're working illegally and therefore don't want to complain or they're so desperate for the work that they think it's better to have any job rather than no job at all. And unscrupulous employers are cashing in on this.

This overcrowded, noisy factory is in a city where, outside, people are eating pepper steaks in expensive restaurants, driving fast cars and earning a fortune. Inside here it's a different picture; it's like something from another age, rows and rows of women sewing clothes in a factory down a back alley just off a fashionable shopping street. This is what you call sweatshop labour: people working unimaginable hours, for half the minimum wage. I talked to a girl here, let's call her Janine, she's 14 and instead of going to school, she comes here to work to earn money so that she can help out with the finances at home. At first she'd intended to do it for just a couple of weeks during the holiday, but when she suggested that she might leave, her boss told her that if she left, he'd report her and tell the authorities that she'd lied to him about her age. And of course, the more school she missed, the harder it was to go back. A vicious circle.

7 There are two sides to this argument; one is that if malpractice is exposed, it cannot continue, and the other is that malpractice will be driven underground.

Connecting words

The language here is covered on page 176 of the Grammar folder.

Go through the information in the Corpus spot, reminding students to be careful when using *and* or *but*.

1 Remind students to read through the article first before filling the gaps with the connecting words from the box.

> **Answers**
>
> | 1 | as | 6 | even |
> |---|----|---|------|
> | 2 | because | 7 | but |
> | 3 | Then | 8 | And what's more |
> | 4 | So | 9 | In all |
> | 5 | Despite | 10 | By then |

2 Students discuss these questions to round off the section.

Writing folder 10

Articles

1 Students discuss where the sentences come from and which parts of the sentences lead them to make this decision.

Answers
a report (topic, phrases like *In conclusion*, fairly formal, very clear language)
b article (topic, rather literary vocabulary like *balmy*, *chugged*)
c article (informal style, e.g. *never in a million years*, use of suspense)
d report (topic, formal vocabulary, e.g. *ascertain*)
e article (topic, rather informal style)

2 Students discuss the differences between articles and reports and complete the table with a partner.

Suggested answers

	Articles	Reports
Who it is usually written for	a wide audience who you don't know and who will only read it if it catches their interest	a boss or some other person in authority
What its aims usually are	to interest, entertain or inform readers	to inform
Any special characteristics of its layout	will usually have an eye-catching title and subheadings	informative title and subheadings; may use bullet points in order to make its structure clearer
Any special characteristics of its register	may be any register – it depends on the readership	neutral or formal
Any other special characteristics of its style	the writer will try to be interesting, amusing or original in order to catch and hold the readers' interest and attention	must be absolutely clear and ambiguous in what it says; usually has a clear introduction presenting what it is going to say and usually comes to some distinct conclusion at the end

3 Students discuss the exercise in pairs before comparing answers with the class as a whole.

Answer
A Lucky Escape sounds far more dramatic and interesting than *My Holiday*.

4

Answers
1 a sounds more intriguing than 1b. It seems more likely to make the reader continue reading. The use of inversion is effective in 1a.
2 a is much more interesting. 2b is rather boring as an opening sentence. The use of a question in 2b helps make for an effective opening sentence for an article.
3 b is better because it uses much more vivid and interesting vocabulary.

5

Answers
Sentence b is a much stronger closing sentence. It is not a good idea for the writer to comment that they themselves feel they haven't done a very good job.

6 Discuss the task fully with students before asking them to write their article. Make the point that students must read the task extremely carefully and highlight all the key points to deal with before beginning their article. Draw attention to the Exam information box.

Point out that the Writing test (Paper 2) is a test of reading as well as of writing. Having discussed the task fully in class, students write their article at home. When marking, penalise candidates if they miss out any of the elements of the task.

25 Intelligence

Genre: Texts dealing with theory

GENRE: Texts dealing with theory
TOPIC: Intelligence and studies

Speaking	Intelligence
Reading	Researching intelligence
Vocabulary	Research and experiments
Grammar	Complex sentences and adverbial clauses
Listening	Different types of intelligence
Workbook contents	
Reading	Two extracts on intelligence
Grammar	Complex sentences and adverbial clauses
Use of English	Part 5 – key word transformations

Student's book pages 154–157

Lesson planning
SV   The Vocabulary section could be given for homework.

Speaking

1   Ask students to work with a partner and discuss questions a–c. The pictures are provided to generate ideas and stimulate discussion.

Reading

1   Ask students to discuss what sorts of questions a horse might be asked and by whom. The answers are all revealed in the text.

2   Ask students to read the first part of the extract.

3   Encourage students to be inventive about how Hans might have answered the questions, before going on to the rest of the text.

4   Encourage students to draw on their own experience when answering these questions.

Encourage discussion and ask students to justify their opinions. Students might say that people today tend to want things to be scientifically proven before they will believe them.

Vocabulary

1

Answers
1	systematic	6	establish
2	investigate	7	procedure
3	observe	8	consider
4	involve	9	illustrate
5	influence	10	distinguish

2

Answers
a 2   b 1   c 9   d 5   e 6   f 4   g 3   h 8   i 7

3   Ask students to do the multiple-choice questions on their own first. They can check their answers with a partner before you go through the correct answers.

Answers
1 B   2 A   3 A   4 D   5 C   6 B   7 C   8 A
9 D   10 B

4   Point out that all the gapped words collocate with another word in the text. Sometimes the word appears before the gap, sometimes after. Encourage students to notice collocations every time they read or listen to a text like this.

Answers
1   prove beyond (all) doubt
2   come as (no) surprise
3   forecast a result
4   incredibly accurate / accurate prediction
5   demonstrate intelligence / above-average intelligence
6   simple procedure / follow a procedure
7   controlled experiment / scientific experiment
8   lack of evidence / concrete evidence
9   cast doubt (over)
10   learn from (your) mistakes

Complex sentences and adverbial clauses

The language here is covered on page 176 of the Grammar folder.

1 Go through the introduction to complex sentences and adverbial clauses. Discuss the examples of the different types of adverbial clauses with students. The examples cover adverbial clauses of time, place, manner, reason and condition. Point out the use of the conjunctions *every time*, *where*, *by*, *because* and *if*, which signal what type of information will follow.

> **Suggested answers**
> The adverbial clause gives more information about:
> a **how often** something happened.
> b **where** something happened.
> c **how** something happened.
> d **why** something happened.
> e **a possible situation** and its **consequence**.

2 Refer students to the Exam spot at this point. Ask students to complete the sentences as appropriate.

> **Suggested answers**
> a he could predict football results.
> b someone other than his owner asked the questions.
> c he could not see the questioner.
> d carefully observing what happened.
> e many people were suspicious of his owner and his act.
> f he could see them.

3 Students can compare their sentences in pairs or in small groups.

Listening

1 This opening activity encourages students to think about what intelligence is, and whether there are different forms of intelligence. When students have finished discussing the questions, get feedback from the whole class. Point out that 'emotional intelligence' is defined as the ability to understand the way people feel and react. This can be used to make good judgements and solve problems.

2 **2 24** Play the recording. Students check their answers with a partner. Get feedback from the whole class and ask students which person they feel they sympathise with most.

> **Answers**
> a 3 b 5 c 1 d 2 e 4

Recording script

Speaker 1: I was really intrigued the other day when a friend of mine told me I had good 'emotional intelligence'. EQ. Not IQ, but EQ. I'd never heard of the term so I asked her what she meant. She said that whenever she was feeling a bit down, I seemed to say exactly the right thing to cheer her up. She remembered the time she didn't get accepted on a course she'd applied for and said that I'd come up with good suggestions about what to do – and actually she did get on the course later! I think it's true that I can tell what people are thinking or feeling even before they say anything. I'm sort of 'tuned in' to people.

Speaker 2: At college, I've noticed most people, when they meet, they kiss each other on the cheek or hug each other. And, well, I mean, it makes them seem really friendly but I feel a bit awkward when they expect me to act like that too. I don't know if it's a man thing or whether it's just me but it's just not my thing to hug or kiss when I meet someone. I never know what to do anyway – kiss on both cheeks, or just one? And which one? What's the rule? Why doesn't anyone teach you this kind of thing?

Speaker 3: It's interesting, my brother, who's a doctor, can never remember my birthday. If he's smart enough to become a doctor, why does he struggle with a simple date every 12 months? Someone once told me 'there's more than one type of intelligence', which explains a lot. Some people have a visual intelligence – they need to see information to be able to understand. There are auditory learners – they can absorb information best by listening to it. And then there are kinaesthetic learners who need to physically do something in order to learn. I did a quiz once, and it turns out I'm mainly visual and but also kinaesthetic. I doubt whether this would help me find the quickest way of studying anything, but we'll see.

Speaker 4: I once took an intelligence test. Lots of numbers and shapes. I gave up after ten minutes. How is that supposed to measure my IQ? Maybe if you do enough intelligence tests, you become good at them, and then you get a huge score. I'm not good at numbers anyway. My wife is. She's like a human calculator. Ask her to write something, though, and she panics. She doesn't have much confidence when it comes to writing. Maybe someone said she wasn't good at it once, and she never bothered developing it. Some people are hopeless at reading maps, my mother for example, but my dad can't understand why she can't use one. Does it mean my dad is more intelligent than my mum? I don't think so.

Speaker 5: When I hear a song, once I've heard it just a couple of times, I can remember all the words. It's like a photographic memory, but with sounds. But I don't know whether it's the actual sounds, or it's just because when I hear a song, the music communicates a certain feeling and maybe that's what I latch on to. I get caught up in it and the words get attached to that feeling. It's like when people can remember exactly what music was playing at important times, like a soundtrack to their lives.

3   Ask students to decide which topic they most agree or sympathise with. If necessary, elicit summaries of each topic first and write them on the board. Play the recording and ask students to make notes only on their chosen topics. Then give students about five minutes to plan how they will present their topic. Encourage them to add their own ideas and to give details from their own knowledge or experience. Put students in pairs or small groups to present their topic to each other. Encourage them to ask questions to find out more information.

4   This question gives students the opportunity to discuss their feelings about the exam, and to focus on any preparation they might need to do. After students have finished, get feedback from the whole class to find out a general view about students' feelings.

Units 21–25 Revision

Student's book pages 158–159

Topic review

Ask students to work with a partner to discuss questions a–j. The aim of this exercise is to encourage students to recycle the vocabulary and structures they have covered in the preceding units in a personalised way.

Vocabulary

1 Ask students to work with a partner and complete all three sentences in each set with the same word.

> **Answers**
> a test
> b drive
> c path
> d gap
> e ease

Grammar

1 This activity consolidates the work students have done on connecting words. Ask students to work with a partner. They should read through the text first, then look at the underlined words and decide which category each connecting word belongs to.

> **Answers**
> *while* = concession and contrast
> *also* = listing
> *that's why* = result
> *to summarise* = summing up
> *as* = cause and reason

2 Answers will vary according to which connecting words students remember from previous units.

Reading

1 Ask students to read the text to find out about the different roles people play.

2 Ask students to match the statements with the different types of team members.

> **Answers**
> 1 diplomat
> 2 challenger
> 3 innovator
> 4 challenger
> 5 innovator / diplomat
> 6 judge
> 7 expert
> 8 expert
> 9 judge/diplomat

3 Encourage students to give a personalised response to questions a–c.